THE ROOKIE'S GUIDE TO MONEY MANAGEMENT

How to Keep Score of Your Finances

THE ROOKIE'S GUIDE TO MONEY MANAGEMENT

How to Keep Score of Your Finances

by Carolina Edwards and Ray Martin

Random House, Inc.
New York   1998
http://www.randomhouse.com

Princeton Review Publishing, L.L.C.
2315 Broadway
New York, NY 10024
E-mail: info@review.com

ISBN: 0-679-77882-9
ISSN: 1093-9865

Editor: Evan R. Schnittman
Designer: John Berdgahl
Production Editor: James Petrozzello
Production Coordinator: Matthew Reilly

Manufactured in the United States of America on recycled paper.

9 8 7 6

Dedication

To Jeff, Tim and Doug.
If the measure of a life is love,
my brothers have made me wealthy
beyond all human calculation.
—C.E.

To Augusta, my loving wife, who
gives me the confidence to follow
my dreams, the child we are expecting,
who gives me hope for the
future, and to my dog Otis . . . he makes
me laugh.
—R.M.

Contents

Acknowledgments

We are deeply grateful for the generous contributions of three experts quoted extensively in this book. They are Magda Polenz, M.D., Suzanne Currie, and Diana Nichols.

Most of all, three very dear friends, Tom Mann, Emerson Bruns, and particularly Ellen Sherberg, stepped forward with assistance during critical points of the book's development. Thank you from the bottom of my heart.

We are indebted to the following people who contributed in different ways to this project. They are: Shirley Alston, Jane Barnett, Andrea Levitt Baum, Kathleen Byrne, Alvin and Libby Dyer, Yanira Fanerte, Jerry and Marianne Franz, Paul Freeman, Harry Halaco, Irene Herrera, Andy Huey, Gina Jacobs, Chuck and Maggie Karkabe, Jennifer Kushell, John Lankenau, Gary Lombardi, Doug Long, Ph.D., Claudia Lopez, Rufus Matin, Peter and Karen Meizels, Darlene Miller, Christina Moore, Chrystal Murphy, Jack and Cathy Strobel, Judy Twersky, and Frank and Paty Viverito. Until you're better paid, our sincere gratitude.

Also, to all the terrific folks at NBC *Today*, particularly Jeff Zucker, for giving Ray the opportunity of a lifetime, and to three exceptional people at the William Morris Agency, Larry Kramer, Henry Reisch, and Mel Berger.

Finally, both of us appreciate the hard work and creative input of the people at the The Princeton Review—John Katzman, and Evan Schnittman—as well as their colleagues at Random House, Peter De Giglio and Kathy Schneider.

Introduction: How To Use This Book

Is your life a mess? Congratulations! You've just taken the first step toward restoring order. Redesigning your financial life (and it will be ready for the cover of *Architectural Digest* by the time you finish this book) will give you an enormous feeling of control over your life. Then the only thing left to do will be the hall closet, right?

The first thing to know is that *The Rookie's Guide to Money Management* was written in a specific order. If you read a book like Carolina's mother does—starting from the front, skipping over large chunks—you may find yourself heavily invested in the Danish stock exchange before you've opened a checking account. Stick with convention just this once, okay?

Equally important as reading this book from front to back is perusing the extensive "Encyclopedia of Financial Terms." This "Encyclopedia of Financial Terms" comes to you from two important sources. Key terms come to you courtesy of *Barron's National Business and Financial Weekly*. (The reading is not nearly as dry as you might think—check out the definition of a Bo Derek stock for instance.) Additional terms come from *The Princeton Review: Word Smart for Business* (Random House, Inc. 1997) by Paul Westbrook.

We place a significant emphasis on financial terms here because, for better or worse, money has a language all its own. The heavy use of terminology has probably been the single biggest weapon in scaring people away from the subject of money and finance. Be brave. You won't have to become fluent overnight, but it will help to get your ear accustomed to the dialect. Actually, you probably already know more than you think.

We feel very blessed to have on this All-Star team three people who bring enormous expertise to this book. Suzanne Currie, a financial planner who helps us with retirement; Diana Nichols contributes information we all want about how to improve our credit and eliminate debt; and Magda Polenz, M.D., a Manhattan-based psychiatrist, generously shares her insights on money and sex—two subjects which are more intertwined than you might think.

Also, you will notice that throughout this book there are mild references to sports terms, used mostly as a structure for the book or a reference point. We've tried not to make anyone nauseous with the analogy. There are similarities, between winning a game and successful money management.

Finally, we have a list of *Le Musts*. It's not long, but it will cut deeply into the list of "things I learned the hard way."

Bon Voyage!

Le Musts

- Health Insurance

- Renter's Insurance (unless you own a home)

- Quicken (unless you are computer illiterate and prefer to stay that way)

- TurboTax (unless you have a brother who is a genius and does your taxes for free)

- Membership in the American Automobile Association, assuming you have an automobile.

CHAPTER 1

How To Finance Your Life

This book was written on the premise that you have just finished your formal education and are about to venture into the real world where you will earn money to support yourself and, perhaps, a family later on. If you're at a different point in your life, please keep reading. It's never too late to refresh or upgrade one's money management skills.

In a perfect world, you are a financial virgin with a clean, debt-free slate, and you are anxious to form good money management habits for life. If you're not, don't worry. In later chapters you'll learn how to work down any debt you may have acquired. What you need now is a plan, a winning game plan, that will guide you through the next seventy years or so. It will incorporate your short- and long-range goals, an approximate time frame for these goals, and ways to finance your dreams.

Don't panic. You do not have to plot your life's course year-by-year or dollar-by-dollar for the next seven decades. The idea here is to get a grip on what kind of life you think you might want—a sheep rancher, corporate lawyer, and mother of eight require different game plans—then set the financial plans to make those dreams happen. You chose a major, took the necessary courses, and got a degree; you can do this.

There are six steps for developing your winning game plan. They are:

1. *Establish a vision of what you want your future to be.* For example, do you see yourself married with children? Or, do you envision an Auntie Mame life-style?

2. *Create a personal time line and highlight the goals that come with a price tag.* Finding the perfect mate doesn't cost much, but an apartment overlooking the Riviera does.

3. *Determine where you are in your finances right now.* In a minute, we'll show you how to find out what your net worth is—that's the amount of your total assets less your total liabilities. This dollar number is what you're left with at the end of the day after you've subtracted your debts. With your goals clearly defined, you will move to *The Manage-to-Grow Money System.*

4. *Develop a budget that covers your expenses and helps you begin to save for your dreams.*

5. *Build a significant nest egg that will protect you when bad things happen.*

6. *Begin to "grow" more money through investments.*

The first three steps will be covered in this chapter. Steps Four through Six make up what is called the Manage-to-Grow Money System—an easy, three-step program that shows you first how to effectively manage the money you have, then how to use some of your money to grow more money. Sounds like a gardening show, doesn't it? The specifics on how to set up a budget you can actually live with and how to build a nest egg will be in the next two chapters. How to begin *growing* more money through investing will be discussed in Chapter 10.

How To Visualize Your Ideal Life-style

So, Step One is to develop a vision of what you want your future to be. Vision, or the ability to see how the big picture may develop, is a key element of success. One of our favorite examples of someone with enormous vision is Ted Turner, the never-boring vice chairman of Time Warner, Inc. and, in case you didn't know, the person responsible for bringing us cable television. When he started his cable business over twenty years ago out of Atlanta, Turner was ridiculed unmercifully nationwide. "Why would anyone pay for television when they already get it for free?" his critics roared. Turner could not be dissuaded from his vision, and today, even people in the tiniest fishing villages off the coast of Chile tune in to CNN.

How often have you said to yourself, "Someday I'd like to do this," or "Before I'm thirty, I want to accomplish that"? Well, the time has come to put all those mental wishes on paper and see how many of them you can make happen. Like Turner, you need a dream, a personal vision, for the prime earning decades of your life. Don't worry, no one will hold you to this—it's just a starting point. Once you have this picture in your mind, then you can lay out a plan on how to pay for it.

Do you think you will marry and start a family? Do you see yourself moving to Paris within the next two years to study art? Is taking a job in New York City and enjoying the club scene for the next few years your childhood fantasy? Think about where you see yourself for the next five years, then determine any steps you might want to take beyond that.

Depending on what kind of person you are, choosing a life-style will either be really easy or really difficult. Judy, for instance, grew up in Seattle and says she knew from the time she was eight years old that she wanted to be a career woman in New York City. Before her fortieth birthday, she had established her own very successful public relations agency in the Big Apple.

Like Judy, you may have known since the age of eight what kind of life is right for you. However, most people find it hard to visualize what they'll want and need twenty, forty, and sixty years down the road.

Be realistic. Remember, there's a wide range of life-styles between Al Bundy's and Donald Trump's. Give it some serious thought; every life-style has its pros and cons.

Here are a few questions you may want to ask yourself:

- What makes you a mentally healthy and happy person? If you draw great serenity and inspiration from the ocean, you may want to save for a summer house at the beach. If traveling makes you happy, you'll have to find a career with a salary and schedule that allows you to spend three weeks exploring the Galapagos Islands.

- Where do you want to live? Is there a particular city, state, or region where you feel most at home—a place where the life-style is you? Do you want the nightlife and cultural attractions of a city, or would having a garden or nearby ski trails make you a happier person?

- Do you want a spouse and children?

- What do you want to do for a living? Theoretically, if you're out of school, you've made this decision or at least given it some thought. Do what you love. Otherwise, you'll just be serving time for the next forty-plus years.

- How long do you see yourself in your current career? Remember, trends show that most people in their twenties will change careers three or four times in the course of their lives.

- What is your potential earning power? The pay scale for a high school English teacher differs from that of an electrical engineer. Look around at the people in your field who are ten years older to get an idea of where you might be financially.

- Do you currently have or anticipate having financial family obligations? Are you an only child with aging parents or do you have a sibling who requires special care?

When you're finished soul-searching, it's time to make a game plan.

How To Sketch Out A Time Line

Take an evening when the *X-Files* isn't on and sketch out a personal time line—for your eyes only—that earmarks certain goals you have, like marriage, children, or sponsoring your own race car at the Indy 500. This will be a sort of vertical *grocery list* of your dreams. Remember, this personal time line is for you alone. No one else needs to see it, so don't be afraid to put your wildest thoughts on the list. Do you want to endow a wing of your local hospital in your family's name? Put that down. Would you like to celebrate New Year's Eve 1999 in New Zealand with a few of your closest friends? It goes on the list. This is how people begin to turn their dreams into realities.

Another benefit to formulating a time line and overall game plan: Numerous studies have shown that if you have a game plan, your goals have a better chance of becoming a reality when you write them down. The simple act of writing down your dreams is a conscious commitment to making them happen. It's worth a try, isn't it?

Ready to begin? Good! The starting point on your time line is now, and you should carry it through age seventy-five or so. It's a little mind-boggling to form your vision of the next six decades, so try breaking it up. Where do you want to be when you're thirty? Forty-five? Sixty? Seventy-five? Among the significant events that you may want to include on your time line are getting married, purchasing a home, having children, and retiring.

Now look at the events on your time line. Which ones carry a significant price tag? Buying a home will probably be your single biggest purchase and will require a significant down payment. Marriage will represent a short-term cost if you are responsible for part or all of the wedding or honeymoon. And, if your spouse does not work, it will also represent a significant long-term change in your financial responsibilities. Likewise, having babies incurs many years of expenses.

The reason for attaching a dollar amount, however vague, to each appropriate entry is this: When you set up a budget, you'll want to anticipate how far in advance you will need to start saving for a particular item or goal. For instance, if you are headed for graduate school and then hope to join the Peace Corps for a two-year stint abroad, now is probably not the time to be socking away bucks for a down payment on a house.

On the other hand, maybe you're gainfully employed and starting to wonder why you are paying nearly $800 for a one-bedroom apartment when your best friend and his wife scrimped for a year, came up with a down payment, and now pay $550 a month toward the mortgage on a two-bedroom house. Not only are they building equity, but, more importantly, there are no neighbors blasting the stereo just above the bedroom.

So, look at your time line again. Maybe you will want to move the "buy house" marker from age thirty to twenty-eight.

It may seem odd to think about retirement when you've barely stepped into adult life, but your game plan won't be complete unless it includes those golden years.

Most working people in the twentieth century have held jobs for forty-four years and retired at sixty-five. This will probably be the standard formula well into the next millennium. However, trends show that exceptions to this rule are no longer exceptional.

Early retirement used to happen only in cases of physical disability or company downsizing, but in the late 1990s, more people are opting for early retirement for a variety of reasons.

Joe is a good—and inspiring—example. By the time he turned forty, Joe was the head of a multimillion-dollar manufacturing enterprise. Two tragic events, the deaths of a child and a close friend, inspired Joe to reexamine his life. He decided his current course was not making him happy, and he walked away from all the perks and bonuses to take a job he loved heading an arts and library council.

While he was making less money in the arts, a critical financial advantage of the job was that it had an impressive pension plan. With careful planning and key investments, Joe retired ten years later. He and his wife now live carefully and comfortably. He does volunteer work and serves as a board member for his favorite causes, and several times a year, Joe plans an Indiana Jones-type adventure to an exotic location.

If retiring before sixty-five is appealing to you, understand that it comes with a very high price tag. If you want to do it, put it in your game plan and start working toward it now.

Regardless of where you pin the stop work marker on your time line, there are the four distinct financial levels you will go through before retirement (see sidebar).

How fast you move through the four levels will depend largely on your income and your ability to invest money. If you are starting a career as an actor or you're a heart surgeon with a long residency ahead, you may spend ten years at Level 1, then speed through Levels 2 and 3, and move to Level 4 by the time you're fifty. (Well, it's a pretty thought.) If you're a newspaper reporter, a teacher, a nurse's aid, or you grow sprouts for a living, you may still be at Level 2 when it comes time for retirement.

Personal Financial Growth Chart

Level 1: Survive independently

Level 2: Build security with a nest egg

Level 3: Grow wealth through investments

Level 4: Reap the benefits of your hard work

Remember, your salary graph over the years will not start at $0 and zoom directly to $124,000 over ten years. There will be plateaus and possibly even periods of unemployment in the line. Most likely you will spend more time on one level than another. However, the object of your winning game plan is to get to Level 4 just as fast as possible!

Where Are You Now?

Okay, so now you have your eighty-year-vision and expected life-style in mind. You understand the four financial levels you'll have to move through, and you've set your stop work marker somewhere on your ideal time line. You know where the finish is—at least, where you'd like it to be. Let's go back to the starting line and see where you are right now.

First, determine where you are in terms of finances at this particular moment. It's a bit more complicated than merely checking the cash in your wallet. What we want to find out is what your current net worth is. Here's the drill to determine net worth:

How to Determine Net Worth

1. Under the heading "Income," list all monies coming in on a monthly basis. This includes your gross salary (gross is the total amount of money you are paid; net pay is what you're left with after taxes, social security, and other deductions are taken out), interest from investments, checks from your parents or Grandma, and what you pick up from redeeming aluminum cans—everything.

2. Under "Expenses," list everything you spend money on, including monthly credit card and loan payments, income taxes, rent, utilities, car payments, gas, entertainment, clothing, and cable TV.

3. Subtract your expenses from your income and hold on to that number for a minute.

4. Next, list all your assets. This includes your cash, the money in your checking and savings accounts, stocks, bonds, your car, house, and personal property. It should not include your collection of shells from Bermuda, but include anything of significant resale value —not what you paid but what you can get for it—like a dirt bike, sewing machine, or camera equipment.

5. Then list your debts, or liabilities. Include student loans, debts to friends and family, credit card balances, plus everything else you owe.

6. Subtract the liabilities total from the assets total. Save this number.

7. Now, subtract your income/expenses number from your assets/liabilities number to determine your precise financial status, or net worth.

8. Is this a positive number or a negative number?

If you have positive numbers, particularly in the income/ expense column, cool. If not, stay calm. You're only on Step 2 in your mission to create a winning game plan that will improve your bottom line. Stay tuned for the next chapter, where we'll figure a way to change that negative into a positive number.

A Rookie's Five Golden Rules

All you need now is strategy. In the coming chapters, we'll talk about some of the best financial planning strategies out there, including saving money, creating a budget, planning for retirement, and eliminating debt. As you read on, remember these golden rules. Read them. Embrace them. Tattoo them on the back of your wallet. They are:

1. Get a Financial Religion.

Believe in effective money management. Trust that it will bring you all the wonderful things you deserve, plus give you the freedom to do what you want when you want. Make it a priority. Set up a routine that enables you to monitor where your money is at all times and where it's going. Do this once a week, if not every few days. Know within $5 where your checking account, credit card, and savings account balances are. Stand vigilant at the door of your wallet and let no penny slip out unintentionally. If you control your money, it won't control you.

2. Emotion is the Enemy.

We all make big and small decisions based on emotion rather than common sense, and often, that's okay. When was the last time anyone chose a name for their new puppy based on common sense? However, try not to buy a $1,000 suit just to impress the cute salesclerk, a car because you adore the color, or a house because you love the wallpaper in the entrance hall.

Here are some other ways money and emotion can be a volatile combination:

Money as medication. You just saw your ex's engagement announcement in the paper, and you're thinking about how much better you would feel if you bought $140 worth of new CDs.

Self-medicating with money is the single most popular misuse of the green stuff in America. Money is a wonderful salve for hurt feelings, disappointment, and depression. Use it when you absolutely must, but beware. An addiction to this kind of medication is more dangerous than drinking cough syrup for the alcohol content.

Keeping up with the Joneses. Peer pressure, or as a prior generation called it, "keeping up with the Joneses," is another real danger to your financial stability. Trying to keep pace with the Joneses was a stupid idea in the 1950s, and in all this time, it hasn't gotten any smarter. It's okay, even valuable, to have financial role models, but don't feel compelled to splurge for a new Harley just because Jeffrey at the office got one. If you feel you must impress people, impress them with your unshakable self-control and five-figure savings account. That'll knock the socks off anybody!

The same is true with *always* picking up the dinner check, or buying every round of beer when you're with the guys at the ballpark. If you think you're impressing anyone, give it up. You're at risk of being taken advantage of by your so-called buddies. Go buy stock, not friends.

Money as a weapon. It is acceptable to use money as a motivating factor if you are an employer. It is destructive to use it as a controlling factor in a personal relationship. Never forget that the number one reason for divorce in America is disputes over money.

Money as false empowerment. Money does give you a feeling of power, but only if you have enough of it. Buying things can offer a false sense of power, and the need for this rush can become a real problem when purchases start to exceed the ability to pay. The term *shopaholic* is no longer used cavalierly; it is a recognized psychiatric disorder, on par with uncontrollable gambling or addiction to alcohol. Build up a $60,000 nest egg. That's empowerment.

3. And Your Budget Shall Set You Free.

Delete from your memory banks everything you thought you knew about budgeting. Overwrite the information with this: A budget is not a diet, a report card, or the terms of your parole. It is your game plan, the one that will help you win the financial game. Do not curse it, hate it, or betray it. It is your ticket to real financial freedom.

4. Keep Your Eye On the Ball.

Whether you are a fan or not, most of us can appreciate one great aspect of football—the scoreboard. Of any game there is, the football scoreboard offers one of the best systems for keeping score. The scoreboard tells you, at any given moment in time, exactly where you are, how many yards you have to go for the next down, and how many points you need to win the game. You know your short-term goals, your long-term goals, and how much time you've got to accomplish them.

Your budget is your scoreboard. It will help you focus on where the first downs are, whether to pass or throw, and, in later chapters, what to do when the ball is fumbled. It's fabulous!

Nevertheless, don't lose track, even for a day, of why you're really playing this game. Is your ultimate goal to provide a comfortable life for yourself and your family? Do you want to be sitting on the verandah of your vacation home, covered with grandchildren, as you peruse your latest seven-figure statement from Smith Barney? That's a pretty vision, isn't it?

In the end, it is your dreams—no matter what they are or how often they change—that soften the crunch of the bullets you must bite to make them happen. Keep them close to your heart, and closer to your billfold, so you never forget what is really important to you.

5. Debt is a Cancer.

Like to watch ice cream melt and run into the gutter? That's what debt does to your hard-earned pesos. If you have credit card balances in four or, God-forbid, five figures and you're only paying the minimum amount due each month, you are hydroplaning into a financial abyss. Do not delude yourself into thinking you are successfully treading water. Wrong, wrong, wrong. That $20 payment doesn't come within a light-year of paring down your balance.

You think it's painful not to be able to buy what you want right now? How will you feel when you realize you can't pay for what you've already bought? Don't eat the candy bar and you won't have to worry about how to burn off the calories later. Get it?

CHAPTER 2

How To Set Up A Budget You Can Live With

If you're beginning to see the big financial picture and what you need to do to be successful, that's great! You've set short- and long-term goals for yourself, and you've established what your net worth is. The next step in the Manage-to-Grow Money System is to design a budget. This budget will be the single most important guide to where you want to go financially.

Here's the deal: Based on the most recent U.S. Census Bureau figures listing the current median salaries, the average college graduate will earn in the neighborhood of $1.3 million during the next forty years—and this is a conservative estimate. With the combined salary of a spouse, a good pension plan, and/or a house that appreciates considerably, this figure can be much greater.

Of course, a third of this $1.3 million will go to taxes straight-away. At least another third will go toward very basic living expenses like shelter, food, and clothes. That leaves not quite $450,000. And how will that be spent? For too many otherwise intelligent adults, it slips unnoticed through their fingers. There may be a wonderful vacation or two, a nice dining room set, and maybe some gold jewelry here and there, but too much money simply evaporates.

Your budget helps you keep score. Think you already know the score? How often have you left the house in the morning with $50 in your wallet, come home with $4 plus change and absolutely nothing to show for what you've spent? This is why budgets were invented. Holding yourself to a budget goes a long way toward ensuring that fewer handfuls of money don't unintentionally end up in the cash register at Sam Goody.

There are five steps to setting up a budget, and, surprise, you've already completed the first two. **Step 1** is setting specific goals for yourself. **Step 2** is determining where you are right now in your finances.

Keeping An Expense Log

Step 3 is the most tedious, but it is extremely necessary. For about one month (minimum two weeks, maximum two months), write down every cent you spend in an *expense log*. A 59-cent, pocket-sized spiral notebook will do nicely. Use it to make a note of every single penny that leaves your hand. Your first entry is the 59 cents you spent on the notebook. Then, how many quarters did you drop in the laundromat? What did you spend on takeout? Even the dime you dropped behind the seat of your car and can't reach, write it down as spent.

You can't do this for just one day or week. It must be done for at least one month to find what we're looking for. It's boring as oatmeal, but try. You may think you know where your money is going. *We promise* you will be surprised after one month. What you'll eventually see is that you really didn't mean to spend $34 on wrapping paper and ribbon. And we bet you had no idea the $2.20 you spend on gourmet coffee every morning adds up to $572 a year. Over twenty years, this totals more than $11,400 worth of caffeine. Do wake up.

While you are keeping your log, however, continue to formulate your budget as we talk about it in this chapter. In a month, you'll adjust your budget based on what your expense log tells you.

A Note About Financial Resurrection

The first three steps—setting goals, determining your precise financial status, and monitoring your exact spending habits—are more critical than you know. The time will come, hopefully not with any regularity, when you suddenly find your budget is totally out of whack and you are in trouble. This often happens after the birth of a new baby, the purchase of a new home or right after Christmas.

It's called real life, and it is similar to falling off a diet. Just pick yourself up and start again by (1) refreshing your goals, (2) determining your financial position, and (3) logging everything you spend for one month. You will use these same three steps to assess the financial damage and make the adjustments you need to get yourself back on track.

Carry on.

Getting Down To The Nitty Gritty

Ready to get down to the nuts and bolts of budgeting? Good. One note: This book enthusiastically endorses computer software money management programs—especially Quicken. If you have this capability, I strongly urge you to use it now. If you're not a computer person, that's okay. Pencil and paper have worked well for centuries.

Establishing Income

In these next two sections, you're going to formulate a total of four lists, each with corresponding dollar figures. The first is the easiest— a list detailing your monthly income. Obviously it should include your salary, any interest from a bank or investment accounts, the $50 you get each month from your doting aunt, the $18 you pick up for recycling, and any other regular source of monthly income.

Establishing Expenses

These next three lists will be longer. You can do this one of two ways: Either make one long list of every expense you have, then divide it into three parts, or list each item under the correct heading. Here are the three headings for expenses:

1. Core Expenses

2. Everyday "Extras"

3. Long-Term Luxuries

Under "Core Expenses," list *only* the most basic necessities needed to live. This is the can't-live-without-it list. Include things like rent, utilities, transportation (car payments, gas, insurance, public transportation maintenance, etc.), health care insurance (unless it's already taken out of your paycheck), necessary clothes (including laundry and dry cleaning expenses), and groceries. Loan payments, child-care expenses, and alimony payments should also be on this list.

Assign a dollar amount beside each item on your core list. For expenses that fluctuate, like utilities, base your number on an above-average monthly bill. It's always better to overestimate expenses.

The list of core expenses is important for this reason: If there is a catastrophic financial emergency (i.e., you lose your job), this is the list of bare necessities you would cut back to. Cable television probably should not be on this list. Your gym or health club, though, may be essential to you. You're an adult now; these are the kinds of decisions you alone make for yourself.

The second list should be anticipated "extras," such as entertainment (movies, video rentals, dining out, ball games, drinks with pals, etc.), nonessential clothing, your health club membership (if not already listed as a Core Expense), designer haircuts, etc.

The third list should include bona fide luxuries that you need to save for like vacations, holiday, wedding, baby gifts, a new car in two years, etc. Sketch out what these items might be and attach dollar amounts to each.

All done? Good work, but there's one more item to add to "expenses."

The Savings Card

At this moment, you're right smack in the middle of learning how to manage your money in this Manage-to-Grow Money System. Sorry to interrupt, but the key to moving on to the "growing money" part of this system is to include saving money. Therefore, you'll need to add this line item to your list of monthly expenses.

What should that number be? For the moment, make it 10 percent of your pretax monthly income. For example, if you make $24,000 a year, that's $2,000 a month gross, or pretax, income. Ten percent would be $200, right? But relax, nothing is set in stone. Just use this figure for the time being. (In the next three chapters, we'll talk about different kinds of savings. Later, you may divvy up this 10 percent in other ways. Stay tuned!)

The Moment Of Truth

Now comes the moment of truth. Gather your four lists, which include a line item for savings. You should have added up all items and determined your total monthly income from the first list. Now add up your three expense lists to get your total monthly expenses. Then subtract your total expenses from your total income.

$$\frac{\text{Total monthly income}}{\text{— Total monthly expenses}}$$
$$?$$

If this is a positive number, bravo! If it is zero, good. If it is a negative number, don't panic. What you're trying to do is balance your budget. In other words, make the income cover your expenses. Sometimes it takes some tweaking. Take a look at the sample budget.

Rookie's Sample Budget

I. List #1: Total Monthly Income		
	Evan's Budget	Yours
Earnings (gross)	$2,208.00 [$26,500/year]	
Cash from parents	$200.00	
Interest	$ 80.00	
Grand Total Monthly Income	$2,488.00 [$29,856/year]	
II. Core Monthly Expenses (Inflexible)		
Rent, utilities, gas, car	$789.00	
Income taxes	$ 736.00	
Food, grocery, drug store	$240.00	
Car loan	$ 118.00	
Credit card	$50.00	
Clothing, dry cleaning, laundry	$80.00	
Health insurance, medical expenses	$84.00	
Regular savings account	$55.00	
Total Core Expenses	$2,152.00	
III. Everyday "Extras" (Flexible)		
Health club	$22.00	
Entertainment	$130.00	
Miscellaneous	$50.00	
Charity	$16.00	
Total "Extra" Expenses	$218.00	
IV. Long-Term Luxuries		
Down payment for a house	$40	
Vacation fund	$10	
Total long-term luxuries	$50	
Grand Total Expenses	$2,420.00	
Total Income	$2,488.00	
Total Expenses	$2,420.00	
Total Surplus	$68.00	

Uhmmm, what to do with that extra $68? Before you pull out that credit card and head for the mall, read the chapters on building wealth and preparing for retirement.

Using the sample budget, you should be able to create a realistic game plan that has a little room for flexibility. Theoretically, there are places where you can economize further—food, the drug store, dry cleaning, entertainment. Are you guilty of any of the *Top Ten Money Wasters*? There may also be months when you have added expenses, such as Christmas presents or renter's insurance, that you need to add as line items or incorporate in to your short-range savings.

What To Do If Your Income Exceeds Your Expenses

If you were lucky enough to have your income exceed your expenses, congratulations! This is the optimum place to be. Now you're wondering—from an accounting point of view—where to put those "extra" dollars? First of all, forget about running out and buying that new VCR you wanted. In fact, do yourself a favor. Don't think of those francs as extra play money. Think of this money as frequent flyer miles toward your ticket to financial well-being. Sock the cash straight into savings.

There is an attitude—the winning attitude—that will launch you into the money game faster and higher than any other single maneuver you can perform. It's called "saving money." It takes discipline, but if you aim to move every cent you earn, find, win, or steal straight into savings, you will jet-propel yourself to financial success in record time. Don't even think about what you might spend a windfall on, just shovel it right into your savings, and your dreams will race to you.

This was why you wrote down your goals in the first chapter. If you don't know what you want, you're not likely to get it. Maybe sometime this year you really want to get your own apartment and lose that leech of a roommate. Or maybe you'd like to splurge on a new stereo for your car. If it's on your planned wish list, then this is where that surplus goes. Make sense?

What To Do If Your Budget Doesn't Balance

Oops! Do your monthly expenses exceed your monthly income? Don't worry. Probably 75 percent of the population falls into this category. Let's regroup.

When laying down a marble floor, one wrong snip can blow the entire project. Thankfully, your budget is not set in stone. It is meant to be jiggled. First, take a look at your long-term luxuries list. A trip to Europe and airfare to your best friend's wedding in Hawaii may not be possible this year. Ideally, this is the easiest place to snip. If not, then you have to move to the everyday extras list and trim there. Sometimes you'll have to eliminate entire categories; try to cut back just a little here and there.

If adjustments in those first two lists can't pull expenses down to match your income, then you're going to have to take a second look at your core expenses. Is there any fat you can trim there? (Remember, savings does not qualify as fat.) Can you carpool to cut down on transportation costs? Is it possible to bring in a roommate to share expenses?

Once you have balanced the equation so that your income covers your expenses each month, make a blueprint. This is your budget, your road map to a financially sound future!

A budget has to be a living, flexible structure. Keep in mind that few of us have formed a budget that works right the first time. Are you spending less at the grocery store and more on dining out? Are your dry cleaning bills less than expected, but your gasoline more? You have to live with your budget for a couple of months to see where the glitches are, then make the necessary adjustments.

The Rookie's List of Top 10 Money Wasters

10. Thigh Master, Ginsu knives, WonderMop, and other super products

Stop watching television with your credit card in your hand. No infomercials and no more than ten minutes a day on QVC, even during the "Christmas in July" special.

9. Leaving appliances on while everyone is out of the house

At the risk of sounding like your father, you might consider turning off major, electricity-sucking appliances when you leave. It's one of those effective little ways of keeping your monthly electric bill under three figures.

8. Buying additional dealer protection packages on a new car

Now pay attention: You're purchasing a brand new automobile that already has a perfect, state-of-the-art rust-preventive paint job. Are you sure you need that extra guarantee against weather damage? Unless your assigned parking spot is nine inches from the Pacific Ocean, save the $550.

7. Paying for extended warranties on major appliances or electronics

You're not paying attention. See *Money Waster* number 8.

6. Leasing your telephone

Unless you're moving into an apartment for a month before you leave to backpack through Europe, don't lease your phone from the phone company. Go to Radio Shack.

5. Dry cleaning hand washables

Are you dry cleaning simple cotton shells, or even silk blouses? What do you think God invented Woolite for? If you take everything—socks, sheets, T-shirts—to the dry cleaners because it's easier than doing laundry, then count on showing up in bankruptcy court neatly pressed at age twenty-eight.

4. Joining any book, video, or CD club

This is something only an eleven-year-old would do. Guess what happens after you've gotten those 10-selections-for-a-penny and blown off the next twenty-four you're obligated to buy? Don't get your foot caught in this bear trap. If you really want to put dents in your credit rating, run up your charge card at Neiman Marcus. It's much more fun.

3. Paying for premium grade gasoline

The joke's on you, bub. Despite what the glamorous TV commercials report and regardless of what might have been true 15 years ago, new consumer studies say premium gas is a waste of $3–$7 per tank. Want to impress your girlfriend? Get a professional manicure. She doesn't care what kind of gasoline you use, and neither does your car.

2. Eating out more than five meals a week

If you pick up coffee and a Danish to eat at your desk in the morning, grab a sandwich with office pals at lunch, and buy a *value* meal at the McDonald's drive thru on your way home from work, the only good thing you'll have is a spotless kitchen. Beside the fact that this life-style will add twenty pounds per year to your body frame, the convenience of fast food and restaurants can cost you $150–$200 a week. Isn't there something you'd rather do with $7,500–$10,000 year?

Spare me the story about not knowing how to cook. Microwave ovens were in general use before any of you were born. If you can read the back of a Stouffer's box, you practically qualify as a gourmet chef. Start gently with brown-bagging your lunch on Mondays. You'll have the whole day on Sunday to put peanut butter on two pieces of bread. Once you've got that down, try eating a bowl of corn flakes in the morning while the electric curlers warm up. You get the idea.

1. Carrying more than $100 cash in your wallet

Few of us are immune to the myriad temptations brought on by significant amounts of cash in our hot little hands. Do you ever feel as if you've joined ranks with superheroes when you're toting a large wad of moola? You're walking down the street and suddenly, your slightly impaired vision takes on an X-ray-like quality. You can see through concrete and you're spotting bargains on items you had no idea you needed.

Remarkable, isn't it? Squash this heat-seeking, budget-breaking missile stored in your wallet and leave large sums of cash at home or in the bank.

While we're on the subject, how about rethinking your general course here? Fifty years from now when you're watching the sunset from the deck of your winter home in Key Largo, what will you remember? Will it be the magenta dress with perfectly matched shoes? The "deal" you got on the latest toy at Radio Shack? Those darling little candles that float in water? Certainly not. Hopefully you will smile back on the fascinating people who have crossed your path, the wonderful family trips to exotic locations, those spur-of-the-moment spaghetti dinners with good friends, and all of the daring adventures shared with your spouse. Certainly not material things.

There's a good five miles between living like the early Shakers and filling your life with stuff. Try asking yourself this question every single time you take your wallet out: "Do I want to give away a piece of my dream for this?" It will save you millions.

Keep Three Wishes Ready

On your desk or personal calendar, jot down right now three things that you would run out and purchase today if someone surprised you with a check for $500. Would it be a new CD player? Snow tires? The silk scarf you've been admiring in the shop near the office

Then, in two months, look at the wish list again. Nine times out of ten, two of those wishes will not still be on your Top 3 List. You may even wonder what in the world made you think you ever wanted that black velvet throw with the three-inch fringe.

Make another list of three wishes, and check it again in two months. Eventually, you'll come to see that many of the things we think we can't live without become boring to us sooner rather than later. It's a good argument in favor of restraint over instant gratificattion.

Budget Buggers

Think you've nailed down the perfect budget? Watch for these little buggers. They can do more damage than a computer virus:

- Banking fees. Whole range of possibilities from monthly service charges, fees for bounced checks, and—the latest budget wrecking fad—automatic teller machine (ATM) charges. Keep close track or build in a pad.
- Monthly paycheck. Remember, if you are paid once a month, some months you will need your budget to cover five weeks instead of four. Plan ahead.
- Newspaper delivery/Pay-Per-View charges. If you get a morning newspaper delivered to your doorstep, or if you're a professional couch potato, don't be surprised when those charges show up at the end of the month.
- Bridge/Highway Tolls. If you thought that 75 cents a day to cross the faster bridge home was chump change, guess where $195 in nickels and dimes goes every year? And that doesn't count the six trips across you make on weekends. Be sure to factor it into your budget.

CHAPTER 3

How Dreams And Emergencies Are Financed

We are now at everyone's favorite part of money management—saving money. You think this is going to be hard, don't you? You think it might even be painful? Relax. Resisting chocolate chip cheesecake is hard. Setting a broken toe is painful. Saving money is easy and, as you will see later in this book, very profitable.

Next to your budget—your road map to financial freedom—saving money is the second most important key to surviving independently. You begin to build a nest to protect you from life's little emergencies. Once that is established, you can start "growing" money, through investing, to build genuine wealth that will last a lifetime.

But we're rushing to dessert when we haven't finished the main course yet. Let's go back and start with exactly how to save money. You probably already have an idea, but here it is in black and white. The most effective way to save money is:

Put Your Money Where You Can't Spend It.

That's it. Obviously there are some nuances, but those eight words are the rock upon which you will build your nest egg. Physically, where you store the money for your nest egg is immaterial as long as it is a safe place. Most agree that once the nest egg reaches a significant size, say over $100, it's best to put it in the bank. That way, it is safe from any sticky fingers, including your own.

Why Save?

This is a rhetorical question. You know why you should save money. Your nest egg will serve two specific purposes—protection from any unexpected emergencies and financing for the long-range goals you laid out in Chapter 2.

Covering Emergencies

When you were a child, the money you saved in your piggy bank probably went toward things like a Barbie Dream House, video games, and maybe a Mother's Day present. It certainly didn't go to taxes or the electric bill. You grew up thinking that your savings was your slush fund to cover whatever earthly delights Mommy and Daddy forgot to buy.

Take this adorable way of thinking and pack it away with your stuffed animal collection. As an adult, you can eat, drink, think, wear, and say what you want. You now have that right. However, one of the trade-offs for this freedom is that your savings is no longer play money. Now it is your fire extinguisher.

Life is punctuated with large and small fires that have to be put out. You get locked out of your apartment at 2 A.M. and need cash for a locksmith. Your cat needs emergency surgery, and you have to pay the veterinary bill. Your car's water pump goes out on New Year's Day, 600 miles from home, and you have to pay for parts and bribe the mechanic to get you back on the road before the boss starts asking where you are. You get the picture.

Building a nest egg may require untold discipline. Believe me, it's worth it. When you have your nest egg in place, the emotional benefits are wondrous. There is a serenity that comes from knowing you can handle any financial challenge thrown in your path. This is something worth reaching for.

Paying For Your Dreams

Once you've prepared for emergencies, your fire extinguisher can grow into a dream maker. Go back and look at your list of long-range goals. What's coming up first on the list? Did you want to dump that lout of a roommate for a studio apartment of your own? Would you like to start planning a real, grown-up vacation for next summer? Maybe you'd like to trade your mother's old hand-me-down station wagon for something manufactured in this decade? Once you have your 3- to 6-month emergency fund in place, and if you're on track with your budget, you can start to think about meeting some long-range goals.

Savings are the way to incorporate big expenditures into your budget. Are you going to need a new car in a year or so? Is your best friend getting married in Hawaii next summer requesting you to be his best man? Use these financial goals to motivate you in your savings program. Would you like to put $1,000 away in six months? Seven thousand dollars over the next three years? You can do it. Focus on sticking to your budget, and keep socking those extra dollars away until saving money becomes a habit.

There will always be things you need in the future. The day will come when you want to buy a condo, you need a second car, or you have to pay for graduate school. Nail down the system, remove the emotion. You'll reach your goals more quickly than you think.

The following is an example of how your savings might increase over a five-year period. It's based on socking away 10 percent of your gross, not net, income:

Year	Projected Salary	Savings Goal	Plus Interest
1	$18,000	$1,800/year ($35/week saved)	$ 1,847.03
2	$20,000	$2,000/ year ($39/week saved)	$ 3,961.39
3	$24,000	$2,400/year ($46/week saved)	$6,509.53
4	$25,000	$2,500/year ($48/week saved)	$9,240.79
5	$28,000	$2,800/year ($54/week saved)	$12,371.84
Total	$115,000	$11,500	$12,371.84*

*Based on 3 percent compound interest

That's $12,371.84 in five years. Not too shabby, eh? And while it goes straight into savings, this money could be a new car or a down payment on a condo. It's a whole year's rent!

Over the course of five years, there will probably be some emergencies for which you will need to borrow from your savings. But the thing to do, after you've borrowed for an emergency, is double up on payments to repay your loan to yourself. If you do this every time you dip into the nest egg, you are guaranteed to have this money at the end of five years.

Getting Started

As you read in the budgeting section, the rule of thumb for annual savings is 10 percent of your pretax salary. (We're not going to tell you what the average American actually saves.) It would be a bad influence. Use this rule to get into the saving habit. If you think you can manage a bit more, fantastic. If it must be a little less, okay, as long as it's something. Be disciplined about putting some money into savings each week. It is one of the best things you can do for yourself and your financial future.

Time Is Money

How's this for inspiration: According to Frances Leonard in her book, *Time Is Money*, if you are 22 years old and can invest $87 dollars a month at 10% annual return, by the time you retire, you will have one million dollars. (If you are 28 it goes to $159, and at 35, it's $324.) Interested? Inspired? You better be.

Growing The Nest Egg

Saving money isn't difficult; most of us learned at the age of three or four how to drop coins into a piggy bank. What is difficult is finding the inspiration to start saving and then implementing strategies that keep you from falling off the savings wagon. This is where this book can help.

Every payday, put 90 percent of your paycheck into your checking account and drop-kick the other 10 percent straight into your emergency-only, nest-egg-growing savings account. Do it without even thinking about what you might buy with that money. It's called "paying yourself first." Before the bills, before any Saturday-night-dinner-and-a-movie, pay yourself first. (If your employer has direct deposit, you may be able to arrange for the 90/10 split of your paycheck to be deposited in your checking/savings accounts.)

We wish we could take credit for this jewel of financial advice, but we can't. Financial planners have advocated the pay yourself first method for years. The Beardstown Ladies, in their successful *The Beardstown Ladies' Common-Sense Investment Guide*, made it even more famous. It works because you don't feel you are denying yourself something, but that you are, in fact, making yourself and your financial future the highest priority. You are prepared to do that now, aren't you? Good.

How Big Should My Nest Egg Be?

Your nest egg should equal three to six months of expenses. If you are in a job that is seasonal or otherwise high risk, like construction or free-lance television production, or if you have children to support, sock six months of expenses into your savings account where you can get to it quickly when the money is needed. You'll never be sorry.

To get the precise figure you must aim for, multiply your current budget, or list of monthly expenses, by three (or six).

Total Monthly Expenses × 3 = Nest Egg Goal

Once you get to your nest egg goal, you'll sleep better at night because you will have a safety net to cover emergencies. As your monthly expenses increase (and hopefully your salary), be sure to update your nest egg goal. The nest egg that you worked so hard to save for in 1997 won't cut it in 2002. Upgrade it every so often to keep pace with the rising cost of living.

On the other hand, keep in mind that there is such a thing as an overgrown nest egg. One financial planner tells the story of a well-intentioned couple who kept a $170,000 nest egg in a low-interest savings account. When the financial planner gently asked them what catastrophic event they anticipated needing $170,000 in cash for, they were speechless. Remember, our definition of a nest egg is synonymous with emergency fund, not long-term savings. You need both, but first build a solid nest egg to help you glide through the billion financial scrapes you will encounter. So, unless you have seven children to support, there's no reason your emergency fund/ nest egg should run into six digits. There are better places to store surplus money that will earn a much higher rate of interest. We'll talk more about this in Chapter 10.

Do not misunderstand. Never stop saving money. Once you've reached that nest egg goal, the fun begins.

Borrowing From Your Nest Egg

While the purpose of your nest egg is to cover emergencies that come up, in reality, there should be very few emergencies. If you've set up your budget correctly, then most irregular expenses, like new tires, annual renter's insurance, and birthday presents, are already factored somewhere into your budget.

For instance, if you have a car that you depend on to get you to and from work, then you need a line item on your budget for "car maintenance." Each payday, you must put money into this category. Maybe you will spend it for an oil change that month, maybe you won't. Carry any unused portion over to the next month, and so on. Then when your car needs a $232 tune-up, the money is in place.

Savings tip

When you formulate your monthly budget, see if you can cover your expenses on four weekly paychecks. Then, in months where there is a fifth week, put the entire paycheck into your savings, and watch that account blossom.

An emergency might be something like this: You crunch down a little too hard on a mouthful of Rocky Road ice cream and out comes a childhood filling. A trip to the dentist to fill this cavity runs $660. If you don't have dental insurance—which probably would cover only part of the cost anyway—the money comes out of your emergency nest egg.

Keep in mind, however, that when you borrow from your nest egg for the occasional emergency, you must pay back the loan so the nest egg is maintained. The good news is you can work out your own repayment plan—just make it within the calendar year.

Combined Balances

As soon as your nest egg reaches the $500 mark, check with your bank about its rules on combined accounts. With many banks, if your checking account and savings account maintain a total of $500–$1,000 or more, many, if not all monthly service charges are dropped. So, even if you are living on the edge with with your savings account (for the moment, of course), your nest egg in savings will cover the $500 minimum. It could save you anywhere from $10 to $20 or more a month or $120–$200 per year. Check it out.

CHAPTER 4

The Basics Of Debt Management

So far we have reviewed how to set goals, determine financial status, develop a budget, and sock money into savings—all important landmarks down the road to financial freedom. If you've followed along and even tried to implement some of these ideas, you should be feeling better, or at least less confused, about money. If you're not, there is one likely culprit from your past that still haunts you—DEBT. It grows faster than fungus in a steamy shower and is twice as difficult to get rid of. But not impossible. This chapter will step off the financial literacy road for just a moment so we can focus on ways to halt the destructive effects of debt.

Before we jump in, though, are you wondering if you really qualify as a patient in the debt management hospital? Roll up your sleeves and take this test to see:

Financial Reality Check: Are You Aware It's Raining?

- Are you tossing, unopened, all mail that even looks like a bill?
- Do you think paying just the "minimum required" is a good thing?
- Have you stopped answering the phone at home to avoid bill collectors?
- Do you use one credit card to pay off another?
- Are you near, at, or over your credit limit?
- Is money, not your newborn, keeping you awake at night?
- Are you and your spouse fighting more than usual about money?
- Are there moments you feel you're sinking into a black hole?
- Are you eyeing the change in the March of Dimes can at the 7-Eleven?

More than four yes answers means you need to stop and reevaluate your budget. Remember the steps?

1. Review your short- and long-range goals.
2. Determine where you are with the Income/Expenses form.
3. Track every penny you spend for one month.

If you're not far off the budget track, swerve back on. If things have gotten seriously out of hand, continue reading.

Good And Bad Debt

First of all, there are two kinds of debt, and the difference is quite important. The good kind of debt is generally something like student loans, car loans, mortgages, and new business loans. This debt enables you to enjoy certain necessities or capitalize on opportunities when you don't have the cash to pay for them up front. Then there is bad debt. This can come from either a series of bad things happening—loss of job, prolonged illness—or from undisciplined overspending, like running up all your credit cards to the max. Bad debt can bring you to your knees.

Hopefully, your debt is good, or at least controllable. A mortgage, for instance, is a planned debt—one you are theoretically managing as a line item in your budget. No matter what type of debt you have incurred, there is only one tool you can use to pull yourself out of this hole—discipline. A consistent show of disciplined spending and saving will begin to resolve the crisis. Here's how to start:

1. *Examine your budget.* If you do not have a budget, go back to Chapter 2 for instructions on creating a list of your assets and liabilities. You can't hope to resolve anything until you see what money you have coming in, what money has to go out, and what you owe.

2. *Make a list of all your debts.* Be complete. Pretend you're in the confessional and you don't want to leave anything out. You may already know what your credit problems are, but get a current copy of your credit report to be certain you have the most current information. As painful as it is, you must have a clear picture of what the total damage may be. Come up with the dollar amount it is going to take you to get out of trouble.

3. *Determine which debts are most urgent.* Are you in imminent danger of losing your house, car, or only credit card? Are your wages about to be attached? Prioritize your debts. At the top of the list should be (1) the debts that threaten to seriously disrupt your ability to function—losing the car that gets you to work, having your electricity cut off, or getting evicted from your apartment; (2) any accounts about to go to court; and (3) any problems involving back taxes.

   If your debts don't fall under any of these dire circumstances, good. List them according to the interest rate charged, from the highest to the lowest. You can get this number from your statement or by calling the creditor. All things being equal, you'll want to pay off the debt with the highest interest rate first.

   Next, decide how much, if any, of the debt you can pay off immediately in a single cash payment, then create a new repayment schedule for the rest of the bills. Any payment you can scrape together will save you interest and finance charges.

4. *Cut spending.* Put a moratorium on credit card use, and cut whatever fat you can from your budget during this crisis. Try to stay away from the mall, and don't read catalogs. Who needs the temptation?

Also, if you get paid for overtime or there is a second job you can pick up for a short period of time, you should consider this possibility. The quicker you pay off debt, the less interest you'll have to pay, and the faster you will be free.

5. *Work with your creditors.* Did you know that in most cases you can negotiate with creditors and collection agencies to reduce either the payments or the debt itself? You can. Emotionally, many people find it a difficult and humiliating thing to do, but what have we said about emotion?

6. *Plan for your life after debt.* Review the short- and long-term goals you initially laid out for yourself. Motivate yourself with these and with sweet dreams of a balanced budget.

Paying Down Credit Card Debt: How Long Will It Take?

By Ray Martin

Think you're keeping your head above water by paying the "minimum amount due" each month on credit cards? Wrong! That $20 payment may keep a particular debt off the delinquent list, but it does little to eliminate the debt itself. For instance, let's say you owe MasterCard $2,500 on a card that charges 19 percent interest. If you never make another charge on the card, and regularly pay 3 percent (the usual minimum monthly payment) on the outstanding balance each month, it will take you thirty-five years to pay off the full amount with interest. Here are the numbers:

Assumptions

- $2,500 of credit card debt
- 10 percent interest rate
- Minimum monthly payments of 3 percent of outstanding balance
- No further charges are made

	Total Payments Made	Outstanding Balance
Year 1	$831	$2,094
Year 5	3,008	1,032
Year 10	4,250	426
Year 15	4,974	176

How To Negotiate With A Creditor

If the bill is past due (but not in collection), call the credit department and ask to speak with a credit manager. If the debt has been turned over to a collection agency, you should be able to get the name and number of the person handling your account. If that person is not there, you can usually leave a message or speak with another representative. Try speaking with other representatives if they have access to your records. Unless you've established a relationship with one person in particular, it's better to speak with someone unfamiliar with your account than to play another round of telephone tag.

Before you make the call to a creditor or collection agency, be sure to have your most recent statement or letter with all the information in front of you. Use your most professional, businesslike voice, and do not bother with explanations or excuses—these people have heard it all before and they don't care. Immediately get the name and title of the person you're speaking with. Then get to the bottom line, which is how to work out a payment plan you can deal with, fast.

Explain that you need to work out a new repayment plan. If the bill is with a collection agency, be prepared. These people will be less hospitable, and they have heard it all before. Collection agencies are hired as a last resort by creditors who have given up hope, and the agencies get a large percentage of whatever they collect from you.

Chances are, one of two things will happen. Either the collection agent will ask you how much of the original debt you can afford to pay immediately, thus reducing the total debt if you can pay a large lump sum. Or the two of you work out a mutually acceptable timetable for repaying the full amount of the debt. Telephone and electric companies usually will not negotiate reduction of the debt but will work out a new payment schedule.

Again, be calm and professional in your tone, and write down the name of the person you speak with. You may have a similar conversation to the one described above. Or the collection agent may offer you a different deal. If you owe $1,200, for instance, she may be willing to settle the debt for two monthly payments of $475 dollars, thus knocking $250 off what you owe.

If you feel you're being put under too much pressure to make an immediate commitment, tell the agent you have to rework the numbers in your budget and call back in 24 hours. Then call back with an answer.

If this is more than you can handle, think about enlisting the services of a qualified debt manager/credit repair professional who will negotiate with your creditors on your behalf. We'll talk more about their services in the section on bankruptcy.

To get started on the specifics for paying down debt, refer to Debt Repayment Chart and the list of Debt Managers/Credit Repair Advisors.

Obstacles You May Encounter

On the road to recovery you may suddenly hit a pothole. No amount of planning will prevent emergencies of all sizes from popping up. If you've had sufficient time to build your savings, you might be able to soften the blow of a "surprise" expense.

If you find yourself unable to cover a small emergency with money from your savings account, check the list on page 34 for other quick cash sources that may be available to you. For emergencies requiring a larger sum, there is a similar list on page 35. Your goal, of course, is to get through the emergency as unscathed as possible. Then you will need to adjust your budget so the source of your emergency fund is repaid.

Another dangerous rut to be wary of is a certain time of the year or a specific life event that turns up the heat on spending. There are obvious seasonal times, like Christmas or Hanukkah. Retailers push particularly hard during the "Back-to-School" period in late summer and early fall. Spring often is when you break out of hibernation and head for new restaurants and new clothes. Vacations are also notoriously bad times for spending much more than you had planned.

In her June 1995 column for *Glamour* magazine, Barbara Gilder Quint had an even better list of times we tend to overspend:

- You start dating someone new.
- You move to a new city.
- You get a raise.
- You get a new credit card.
- You are planning your wedding.
- You're stressed or depressed.

Just remember, for every good reason to spend, there are three times as many better reasons to save. If you find you are losing your faith as well as your disciplined financial habits—STOP! If you give up on your budget, you might be bussing tables until you're sixty-seven.

Bankruptcy: The Last Resort

The number of people declaring personal bankruptcy has increased dramatically over the last ten years. In its briefest form, here is a summary of what happens: Through a bankcruptcy layer, you go before a bankruptcy judge and declare that you are incapable of ever repaying your debts. The judge decides if your situation is truly beyond repair. If he or she decides it is, then bankruptcy is declared.

This doesn't mean you get to skip out of court a free person. The judge will also decide what part of your assets, for instance your home, car, jewelry, or artwork, can be sold to pay creditors a portion of your debt. If the debt exceeds the cost of your home, you will lose it, plus anything else of value you have that can be liquidated.

Bankruptcy gets creditors off your back and may keep you from going to jail. However, it will also make you a financial pariah for the next seven to ten years. Regardless of what the television ads claim, this means you cannot get a loan for a house or car. Your furniture and major appliances may be repossessed. You won't be allowed to have credit cards. You may have trouble renting an apartment. To pour salt on the wound, all bankruptcies become public record, and some newspapers publish these events as a matter of course. Also, bankruptcy can show up on a routine employment check—not a plus to most potential employers.

Diana Nichols of Gold Key Credit Services in Westchester, New York, advises against bankruptcy except in the most severe situations and particularly for anyone in their twenties. You may be able to avoid it by working with a credit and debt management expert who negotiates on your behalf with your creditors to greatly reduce your debt. Diana's agency, for instance, guarantees it will reduce your debt by 30 percent, but is often able to knock off 50 to 70 percent.

A debt manager usually charges a fee equal to 10 percent to 12 percent of your original debt.

Other Sources Of Help:

Debtors Anonymous

Check your local white pages or write to Debtors Anonymous at P.O. Box 400, Grand Central Station, New York, NY 10163 for a list of chapters in your area.

Credit Cards

If you have access to the Internet, the Bank Rate Monitor's Web site (http://www.bankrate.com) posts a list of low- and no-fee credit cards and cards with low interest rates.

So if you owe a total of $20,000 and the debt manager negotiates it down to $10,000, you will have to pay $2,000 to the debt manager and the remaining $10,000 of your debt. Even so, you've cut your debt by $8,000.

If working with a credit advisor or debt manager isn't enough to solve your problem, find a lawyer who is experienced in bankruptcy. The American Bankruptcy Board of Certification (510 C Street NE, Washington, DC 20002) publishes a list of experienced lawyers. Find out what the lawyer's fee is before you make an appointment to see him or her.

Sources Of Quick Cash In An Emergency

Here are some conventional and unconventional sources of fast cash in cases of emergency:

- *ATM*: Good source of quick cash if you have it in your account. Usually there is a limit (for your protection) on how much cash you may withdraw from the machine per day.

- *Checking plus*: This is a line of credit many banks extend to their good checking account customers. It is really a loan the bank offers you so that you can write a check (or checks) up to a certain amount and the bank will cover them. The loan must be repaid and with interest.

- *Credit cards*: Many credit cards allow you to withdraw some cash against your account. However, remember that the interest charged on this cash advance can be quite breathtaking. Use it only in an emergency and pay it back quickly.

- *Pawn shop*: Most people don't know that this is a highly regulated industry with strict rules for its members. The overly simplistic drill is that your item is appraised, and if you leave it for cash—you must have forms of identification and a verifiable address—you have ninety days to retrieve the item before it's sold. You must be notified in writing prior to the sale that your ninety days are nearly up. The good thing about pawn shops is you can get quick cash, and if you don't repay, it doesn't affect your credit rating. The bad news is the interest rates are higher than those of a bank. But, if your car dies and you have no other source to turn to, this is a good place for a fast loan.

- *Second job*: Does your employer pay overtime? Can you

wait tables, tutor students, type, bake, sew, mow grass, or shovel snow? In larger cities, there are some companies with late shifts requiring data and word processing skills. Also, there is seasonal work available at places like Macy's during Christmas time—employees get a discount on merchandise bought there—or H & R Block during tax time.

Sources Of Large Sums Of Emergency Cash

- Borrow from family or friends. This is not ideal, but it may be necessary in an emergency. To avoid unpleasantness, it is essential that you treat a loan from a friend or relative as carefully and formally as any other business transaction. List the terms of the loan, interest rate, and the repayment schedule. Federal tax laws allow an individual to give a family member up to $10,000 tax free, and a married couple, like your parents, can give up to $20,000 annually. Anything over those amounts is subject to gift tax.

- Take out a loan, second mortgage, or home equity loan. Don't rush into a consolidation loan. The friendly actors in the commercials for these loans want you to think that the solution to all of your financial problems is just a phone call away, but these loans have notoriously high interest rates. They're high because they prey on panicked, debt-crazed people.

- Only as a last resort, borrow from your retirement plan. Check the rules, but in most cases you can borrow money from your retirement plan if you have one. While repayment plans vary, the good news here is that essentially you are borrowing from yourself. In most cases, you have up to five years to repay the loan. But remember, you're borrowing from your future.

Try very hard not to miss any payment. Even if the payment is only $5, it prevents the creditor from putting a black mark on your credit rating. Such marks are hard to explain later and nearly impos-

What Bills To Pay First In An Emergency
- Utilities
- Mortgage or Rent
- Car
- One Credit Card

sible to remove. Remember, you can call and try to negotiate with most creditors for an extension during times of emergency. If you have a record of regular payments, creditors often are more lenient.

The Debt-Free Navigational Chart

Here's an example of how you can set up a repayment schedule. This system uses a chart to show you how to best distribute the amount you can afford to pay each month. Our example shows how you could pay off $5,300 in debts allotting $380 a month. The high-interest bills get paid off first, then the payment gets shifted to the next highest interest debt and so on. If you stick to this plan and don't run up additional debt, everything will be paid off in sixteen months and you will be a debt-free person with no black marks on your credit rating.

Debt Repayment Chart 1					
Creditor	Credit Card #1	Credit Card #2	Hospital	Car	Mom
Balance	$600	$400	$2,000	$1,500	$1,500
Interest Rate	18.9%	16.9%	10%	9%	0%
Month					
1	$84	$50	$112	$84	$50
2	$84	$50	$112	$84	$50
3	$84	$50	$112	$84	$50
4	$84	$50	$112	$84	$50
5	$84	$50	$112	$84	$50
6	$84	$50	$112	$84	$50
7		$100	$146	$84	$50
8			$246	$84	$50
9			$246	$84	$50
10			$246	$84	$50
11			$246	$84	$50
12			$246	$84	$50
13			$98	$232	$50
14				$260	$120
15					$380
16					$350

Debt Managers/Credit Repair Advisors

For professional help with managing debt, look under the heading "Credit & Debt Counseling Services" in the Yellow Pages. Often, this work can be done over the phone, although you may feel more comfortable meeting with someone face-to-face. Like any service, it is vital to get in writing what the fees are, what services will be rendered, and how the fee is to be paid before you begin working with anyone.

There are also nonprofit credit counseling services. The best known is the Consumer Credit Counseling Service (CCCS), which has more than 800 offices nationwide. However, one thing you should know is that this organization customarily is paid a percentage of the loans it helps you to pay off. Therefore, it is unlikely for CCCS to recommend the protection of bankruptcy, even when it is called for.

You can find out the location of the CCCS office nearest you by calling (800) 388-2227. Your Better Business Bureau may be able to give you the names of similar services in your area.

CHAPTER $5

Retirement: How To Save For The Future

I was in the checkout line at the grocery store early one Sunday morning and just ahead of me was a stately, eighty-something gentleman buying a quart of vanilla ice cream. After he had rung up the ice cream, the cashier politely asked, "Is that everything?" to which the gentleman said "Yes." The cashier waited a moment, then gently reached over and pulled out two packages of Kraft Swiss Cheese from the man's coat pocket.

Those of us around him silently gasped. The cashier quietly asked the man if he had anything else hidden, then delicately said "Don't ever do that again," and sent the man on his way. When the man was gone, the cashier shrugged and said, by way of explanation, "Food stamps run out about this time of the month."

Many otherwise intelligent adults save for retirement the same way they studied for exams: Wait until the last moment and cram. That method might have gotten you through school; it won't get you through retirement. It is very hard to be young and financially strapped; don't be in the position where you have to steal cheese at the A&P when you're eighty-two. Start saving for your golden years now.

If it seems to you that retirement planning is getting an unusually hard sell here, you're right. The reason? For someone who is in his or her twenties now, the possibilities are very exciting. With two inches of discipline and a dash of luck, you could retire at sixty-five with a million dollars in your pocket, and that doesn't include the additional income you will have from your savings, Social Security, inheritance, investment portfolio, and your pension plan.

Saving for retirement is so much more effective when you start at age twenty-five than it is if you start at fifty. The reason? Your money—like you—has a longer time to generate more money through the magic of interest. For example, of that million we mentioned, less than half will come from money you actually contribute. The rest comes from the interest your invested dollars earn over forty years.

Why Your Retirement Will Be Nothing Like Your Parents

According to all financial forecasts, your retirement is going to be much different than that of your parents. And no, not entirely because of the Social Security question mark.

Your parents lived in a different age. Chances are at least one of them worked for a large company that offered lifetime security and an impressive pension plan. In addition, the house that they bought twenty-five years ago probably tripled in value and made them a tidy profit when they sold it. Now, they are living in Florida and re-

Where you want to be at age 65

- Kids raised, educated, and married

- Mortgage on house paid off

- Totally debt free

- Enough money invested so that the annual interest payments plus Social Security and pension payments equal 65 to 75 percent of your pre-retirement salary

ceiving generous Social Security checks that will equal about seven times more than what they paid into the program.

You, on the other hand, are likely to change career paths an average of three times in the course of your working life and to switch jobs even more frequently. There will be no pension plan from a single company that you build over many years. Instead, you must be prepared to create your own retirement plan and to take it with you every time you change jobs. Or else.

Similarly, because of the job changes, it is unlikely that you will purchase a new home and watch it grow in value for twenty-five years. Besides, housing prices may not keep pace with inflation.

And finally, there is a debate over whether Social Security and Medicare will have funds available when you retire. If both fail, will the federal government spend the billions to save you that it did to save Mexico and the endangered snail darter? Look to Las Vegas for the line on that bet.

Now stop crying. It's better to hear the truth now and figure out how to deal with it than to be unpleasantly surprised twenty years from now.

How To Start Early (And Maybe Finish Early)

According to Manhattan financial planner Suzanne Currie, the savvy 25-year-old who starts saving for retirement, even modestly, actually stands a good chance of having an easier time of it than his or her parents. "The most important step in retirement planning is to get time working on your side. The earlier you start, the less you'll have to set aside each month to reach your goal," says Suzanne. "Most Baby Boomers made, or are making, the mistake of waiting until their forties or fifties to start planning for retirement. They have to run three times as fast to catch the retirement bus."

Twenty-somethings also have a decided psychological advantage, says Suzanne. "As a whole, they are very realistic about their futures. Generation Xers are asking all the right questions about Social Security and Medicare. They are not naive, and they are not likely to depend on the kindness of strangers or the government for their future."

"Let me emphasize that the pervasive feeling among most financial planners is that compound interest is better than sex," says Suzanne. Compound interest, by the way, is when a financial institution pays you cash on both the money you've invested and the interest it has already earned. Simple interest, on the other hand, pays money only on your principal. Savings accounts generally only pay simple interest, but other accounts, like a money market account, also available at your bank, pay compound interest.

Here are two dramatic examples of the power of compound interest. The first is a riddle of sorts and pure fiction—nobody on this planet pays 100 percent interest.

> If someone offers you the choice of $1 million in cash or one cent compounded at 100 percent daily for thirty days, which should you take?

You took the $1 million cash, didn't you? Big mistake. One cent compounded daily for thirty days comes to more than $10 million (see chart on page 45). Even after you pay the taxes on Mars, it's a better deal.

Here is an example that's a little more realistic:

> Two friends, Scully and Mulder, each start to save for retirement. At age thirty, Scully begins to invest $2,000 a year (the max on an IRA, or individual retirement account) at an annual compounded interest rate of 9 percent. She does this for ten years and then stops.

> Mulder, on the other hand, starts his retirement savings at forty and also invests $2,000 a year in an IRA that pays an annual compounded interest rate of 9 percent and stops at age sixty-four.

The final score? Scully $285,000. Mulder $185,000.

Scully has $100,000 more than Mulder, even though she invested $28,000 less. What made the difference is that Scully's investment kept earning money through compound interest even though she stopped paying into the plan after ten years.

Like to have this kind of success? Here are the steps you can take:

1. Start now.

Put off doing your laundry and do this instead. Even if you can only afford $5 a week, start investing in a retirement plan. You won't have the time factor on your side later, and you will have missed out on earning tens of thousands of dollars in interest. Don't be an idiot.

2. Make retirement a line item.

The most painless way to save for retirement is an automatic investment program called the 401(k) plan. In this forced savings plan, a small amount is deducted from your paycheck each week and put into an investment plan.

Apart from the appealing no-maintenance aspects of a 401(k), two things make it a windfall. First, many employers match every dollar you invest with as much as another 50 cents (are you listening to this?) and second, the money is tax-deferred. It's almost too good to be true. If your company doesn't offer a 401(k) plan, open an IRA.

If the commitment involved in either one of these plans is making you nervous, remember this: It's not like a credit card where you must make a monthly payment. You can reduce your payments to practically nothing. With an IRA, after the initial deposit, you can go indefinitely without paying more into it. This defeats the purpose of course, but in an emergency or tight times, you can suspend payments without penalty.

3. Don't be an investment wimp.

It is unlikely that you will be able to maintain your preretirement life-style on Social Security pension payments alone. Your savings and investment portfolio will be key supplements.

As unlikely as it sounds, the most secure place for your retirement cash is also the most volatile—the stock market. Sure, it can give you a roller coaster ride, but stock is one of the few investments that can survive the ravages of inflation.

According to Suzanne Currie, Treasury notes, generally regarded as the ultimate in security, have earned an average of 4.2 percent, after inflation, over the past twenty years. Over the same period, stocks have generated slightly more than 8 percent interest. (See Stock Market Ups and Downs on page 94.)

4. Examine your withholding taxes.

As a financial planner, Suzanne Currie would never recommend this technique, but if you don't have a 401(k) plan and absolutely cannot make yourself save for retirement any other way, try this: Have extra money withheld from your paycheck by decreasing the number of tax exemptions you take by one or two. Suzanne will say that you're giving Uncle Sam an interest-free loan, and this is correct. But if you've failed to set money aside any other way, this is not a bad way to force yourself to save. When you get your tax refund check next spring, just be sure to invest the income.

5. Get professional help.

If you are just starting out, now may not be the time. But by the time you hit 30, particularly if you have a family, the advice of a financial advisor (not exclusively your Dad) is vital. Continue to read and study, buy *Money* Magazine, take advantage of free seminars, and watch CNBC. Eventually, though, a one-on-one with a fee-based financial planner could enable you to leapfrog to that seven-figure retirement fund even faster.

Financial advisors are like doctors—you may have to visit a few before you find one you have confidence in. There is nothing wrong with shopping around.

How to Roll Over Your 401(k) When You Change Jobs

If you haven't heard the term roll over used in connection with money before, let me point out right away that it has nothing to do with what your mate does after sex, what can happen to a car in a bad accident, or what you need to do with a newborn infant so his head doesn't grow flat on one side. Most often, the term roll over refers to what happens to your employer-implemented 401(k) plan, pension, or retirement fund when you change jobs.

Here's an example: Say you've worked at your current job for four years, three of which you participated (happily) in the company's 401(k) plan which has grown to about $7,000. Then you're offered a great new job (meaning more money) with a different company. You've accepted, and you are about to give your current boss the routine two-weeks notice. A decision far more important than what to do with all those soon-to-be antiquated business cards is what to do with the money accumulated in your 401(k). Before you leave your old job, you will have to tell your employer what you want done with this money. Here are your choices:

- *Cash the plan—take the money and run.*
- *Roll it over into a 401(k) plan at your new job.*
- *Reinvest it into a new or current IRA plan.*

Option number 1 looks yummy, doesn't it? Wrong. Unless you've just had a serious emergency come up, or this is the exact moment you've chosen to buy a house, disregard this possibility right away. Taxes may leave you with less than two-thirds of the original savings, and you will have squashed your nest egg.

The ideal scenario is rolling your money into a similar, if not identical, 401(k) plan at your new job. This enables you to keep what you have and continue socking more money away before you are tempted to spend it on cross country skis. Your new employer may not begin his matching contributions until you've worked there for a period of time, maybe as long as a year. Your original $7,000 will remain in tact; it will be invested and you will continue supplementing it each paycheck as before.

The alternative if your new employer doesn't have a 401(k) plan is to open an IRA and deposit the money there. It will continue to earn interest, you can contribute up to $2,000 more a year to it and there are no taxes assessed.

Exploring The Possibilities Of Early Retirement

Fantasies about early retirement engulf most of us every Monday morning at about 7:10 A.M. But early retirement comes with a very high price tag.

Certain professions—police, armed forces, airline pilots—have either mandatory early retirement rules (usually after twenty years of service) or offer strong incentives to leave before sixty-five. The rest of us have to depend on our financial savvy to consider early retirement.

Investments are the key. At whatever age you retire, your investments must pay enough annual interest to support you and your family. You have to figure out how much to invest each year—at what interest rate—to reach this number. It's a brutal equation to work out and requires more expertise than this book can give. Check with a financial planner.

If early retirement is an appealing possibility to you, keep socking money away in those high-interest investments and see a financial planner, or your friendly, longtime banker, as soon as you can.

The Magic of Compound Interest

Here's a very impressive example of how compound interest works. The Tooth Fairy offers you $1 million in cash or one cent on which she will pay 100% interest, compounded daily, for the next 30 days. Which is the better deal? See the bottom line.

Day 1	$0.02	Day 16	$655.36
Day 2	$0.04	Day 17	$1,310.72
Day 3	$0.08	Day 18	$2,621.44
Day 4	$0.16	Day 19	$5,242.88
Day 5	$0.32	Day 20	$10,485.76
Day 6	$0.64	Day 21	$20,971.52
Day 7	$1.28	Day 22	$41,943.04
Day 8	$2.56	Day 23	$83,886.08
Day 9	$5.12	Day 24	$167,772.16
Day 10	$10.24	Day 25	$335,544.32
Day 11	$20.48	Day 26	$671,088.64
Day 12	$40.96	Day 27	$1,342,177.28
Day 13	$81.92	Day 28	$2,684,354.56
Day 14	$163.84	Day 29	$5,368,709.12
Day 15	$327.68	Day 30	$10,737,418.24

Getting Organized

Here's the score as we approach halftime: You've set personal financial goals, determined your current financial worth, created a budget that you can live with, and you're shoveling money into your nest-egg fund just as fast as you can, right? Fabulous!

In this diverse chapter, we're going to address how to set up, organize, and maintain the financial career you're creating for yourself. Let's start with the most remarkable development in personal finance this century: Your computer!

Managing Your Money With (Or Without) Your Mouse

Our goal in this section is to find a system, a sort of scorecard really, to help you keep an accurate and easily updated record of where all your money is and where it's going.

For centuries, a simple ledger or notebook worked well. In the last five years or so new products have come on the market to help you organize and maintain your personal finances with a personal computer. So now you have two choices: The twentieth-century method of using a pencil and paper works fine. Or the twenty first-century method, where your computer does much of the work, using a personal finance software program such as Quicken.

Here's the factoid that will blow your socks off: Financial planner Ray Martin says that his clients who use Quicken *increase their savings by 25 percent the first year they use the program!!!* One important key, he adds, is to know how to use the split transaction feature. Ray has been known to buy Quicken, take it to the client's home, and install it for the client himself, but don't call him if you live in Fargo.

It's hard to exaggerate the difference between the pencil-and-paper accounting system and a personal finance software program. Where all of us need the most help in our lives is in properly managing two valuable assets: Our time and our money. The very literal-minded computer lends itself perfectly to the detailed-oriented chores of money management.

The new personal finance software programs also offer something traditional financial management methods don't: They're fun! And they may be popular—Quicken is used by more than 10 million people—because they're like a better-tasting toothpaste—it encourages you to brush more often. Using the software makes dreary tasks like balancing your checkbook and paying bills less boring and certainly less frustrating.

If you choose the personal financial software route, keep in mind that it will make things easier and more fun. You just have to plow through the initial set up of the program. Once you're up and running, use financial writer Chris Shipley's handy tips to get the most from your system. The biggest benefit of a personal finance program is the ability to see precisely where your money is going.

If computers are not your thing, or you can't afford one right now, establish a system where you keep all your financial information in one place. This should be a dedicated space where you can spread out and work on your finances. A desk and filing cabinet are good, a large box with folders will work in a pinch. If everything you need is in one place, you won't waste fifteen minutes rummaging around looking for things.

Once you have everything set up, it might take you fifteen minutes a week (seven minutes on Quicken) to run down the weekly list and maybe thirty to forty minutes to go over the monthly list. Be sure to run down both lists whether you're wired or not.

Banking On-line

If you go the computer route for managing your finances, check to see if your bank offers any on-line services. From their home or office, customers can call up their accounts, check balances and recent transactions, pay bills, and even buy stock via their PC. It's truly awesome!

Some banks, such as Citibank, will give you the necessary software and throw in the bill-paying services at no charge. For those that do charge, the cost is usually under $4 a month. You submit a list of payees and corresponding addresses when you sign up. Then, once a month upon your on-line command, the bank issues a check for the amount you indicate. You'll never go scratching around for a stamp again!

You do need to allow the bank three to five days to send out a check, so factor that into your time frame. Mortgage lenders have no sense of humor when it comes to *the check's in the mail* line. A late payment here will affect your credit rating.

If you are not inclined to going on-line with a computer, some banks still offer special services, like the bill-paying service, through the phone banking or tele-banking systems. With a touch-tone phone, you can call your bank and, by pressing certain keys, determine account balances, transfer money between accounts, and pay bills. It's a great way to take care of business, particularly if you travel. Just be sure to record your transactions when you get home.

Yet another system being offered in many parts of the country through aggressive marketing by banks is something called a screen phone. This is a regular phone that also has a small screen—similar to a tiny ATM screen—that lets you see your banking transactions. There is a retractable keyboard, and the screen phone also carries added benefits like Caller ID and/or Call Log. Check with your bank to find out what, if any, monthly charges are connected with this before you sign up.

High-Tech, No-Stamp, Bill-Payment Systems

The mundane chore of paying bills is being made easier by more and more banks. Citibank, Chase Manhattan, Wells Fargo, and many others are changing the way you will pay off your debts in the coming millennium.

In most cases, what you do is provide your bank with a list of the merchants or utilities that you want paid. Each month when you receive your bills, you key in the amount you want sent to each payee—either at an ATM, or via the automated phone banking service—and the bank sends a check. No stamps!

But, there are a couple of catches. Some banks offer the service for free, while others have a nominal (under $5) charge unless you maintain a minimum balance. Be sure to check. If you only have four or five bills a month, a $3 service charge may not be worth it. On the other hand, if it's free, think of what you'll save in stamps.

The more important catch is that it may take the bank as many as five working days to issue the check. If you wait too long, you may get slapped with a late charge, or, worse yet, have your phone service turned off.

Now, if you want to sprint through the bill-paying chores faster than Michael Johnson, try hooking up with your bank on-line. Many offer software that gets you into all your account information as well as the bill-paying service. It's fabulous! Your manage-to-grow system can be cut down to minutes a week! Again, check to see if there are fees involved. Usually, the cost is no more than $3 or $4 a month, which is a lot unless it inspires you to pay your bills more promptly. You could be paying that much and more in late charges.

Record Keeping

Even if you are a five-star pack rat in possession of all your third-grade report cards, the time will come when you'll have to choose between throwing something out or getting a new apartment.

The general rule of thumb for what financial records to save is this: After three years, you can toss most paperwork. However, there are significant exceptions. Here's what the financial experts say about what to keep and what to throw out:

Bank Statements: Hold on to bank statements for three years. These are often needed when applying for a mortgage, which usually requires statements from the past twelve months. You will have to explain any exceptionally large deposits, e.g. gifts from parents, Grandma, etc. The lending bank likes to know how much of a down payment you saved and how much came from sources of income other than your paycheck.

Personal Checks: Save canceled checks for three years. After that, pull checks written for significant purchases such as major appliances, deposits on an apartment, your purebred Yorkshire puppy, alimony payments, or anything else you might need to document payment for later. You should also keep any checks you might need for tax purposes, including those for business expenses or related to interest on investments.

Also, keep in mind that if you apply for a mortgage, some banks will ask you for proof that you've paid your rent—and paid it on time—via your canceled checks. This is another good reason to pay the rent promptly, even if the landlord is your Mom.

Credit Card Statement(s): Once again, save for three years, then throw out everything but those bills listing significant purchases.

Utility/Telephone Bills: If you are in a new home or apartment and you are trying to determine what your average gas and/or electric bills are over the course of a year, save these utility bills. Otherwise, throw them out. You can get copies of past bills from the utility company should you need them later. Old telephone bills come in handy if you frequently lose out-of-state phone numbers of friends and family you've called in the past. If this isn't one of your annoying little flaws, toss them.

Tax Returns: NEVER THROW AWAY OLD TAX RETURNS! This includes W-2 and 1099 forms. These are real keepers because they bring back such happy memories. They may also be very helpful if you need to retrace your financial moves. If you've lost a return, the IRS will send you a copy for a small fee. What you can toss after six years are your supporting tax documents for expenses listed on your federal tax return. The IRS cannot audit your return any further back than six years unless it suspects fraud. So, to be safe, keep the return for seven years. On your state returns, check before you toss. In most states, three years is a good rule, but in some, such as California, you can be audited for four years.

The Three-Year Exceptions:

Keep in mind that canceled checks, bank and credit card statements can be invaluable if you need to document the purchase of an item that has been stolen or is still under warranty and needs repair or replacement. For big ticket items like televisions, VCRs, microwaves, stereos, computers, etc., save the receipt and the check/credit card statement until you've hauled the item out to the curb for pick up.

I.R.S.

In an effort to be nice, the Internal Revenue Service publishes a brochure called "Record Keeping for Individuals," Publication No. 552. Call 800-829-3676, for more info.

You should also keep year-end mortgage and interest statements and property tax bills for your upcoming tax return.

Paycheck Stubs: The experts say three years. In most cases, particularly if all your stubs are from the same employer you can save stubs for twelve months, then keep only the last paycheck stub of the year with the annual totals on it, and toss the rest. The big exception is if you think you might purchase a new home. Some mortgage applications ask for the past twelve months of pay stubs as documentation of your salary and gainful employment.

If You Own A Home: Anything connected with the purchase of a house (deed, title, mortgage contract, etc.) should not be used as a coaster. The best place for these documents, and others listed below, is a safe-deposit box in a bank. Most cost under $50 a year and are well worth the protection. Do, however, make sure another family member knows which bank, in case your elevator falls thirty floors.

An in-wall safe at home is also good, but forget using a metal lockbox for these critical documents. It may keep nosy guests from finding out what you paid for your house, but it's too portable not to walk out the door with a burglar.

If you make any major improvements or repairs on your home, save the documentation (receipts, canceled checks, etc.). These records could help you lower your capital-gains taxes if you sell your home for a profit.

Investments/Pension/IRA: Save all annual statements forever. Toss monthly brokerage, pension, IRA, and mutual fund statements except the dividend-reinvestment statements and trade confirmations. You'll need these at tax time.

Here's a list of other documents, both personal and financial, that you should keep in a safe place. A good idea is to keep the originals in a bank safe-deposit box and photocopies locked in your desk drawer at home. Some of the documents to keep track of, for yourself and your family, include:

- Original birth certificate(s)—safe-deposit box
- Passport(s)—locked drawer at home
- Marriage certificate—safe-deposit box
- Divorce certificate—safe-deposit box
- Household inventory—safe-deposit box & home file
- Medical record(s)—home file
- Original Social Security Card(s)—safe-deposit box
- Military discharge papers—safe-deposit box

- Pension records—home file
- Vehicle title(s)—safe-deposit box
- Vehicle registration(s)—with vehicle
- Trusts—safe deposit box & attorney's office
- Power of Attorney papers—home file & attorney's office
- Insurance policies—home file (policy numbers in safe-deposit box)
- Notes for outstanding loans—locked drawer at home
- Appraisals for art and antiques—safe-deposit box
- Health care proxy—locked drawer & attorney's office
- Living will—locked drawer & attorney's office
- Warranties—home file
- Will—safe-deposit box & attorney's office

One tip on renting a safe-deposit box: Most banks offer two, sometimes three, sizes of boxes. If you own something that is irreplaceable, like your great grandmother's silver or a valuable baseball card collection, consider renting the larger safe-deposit box and keeping the items there. It might be a difference of $5 to $7 a year, which is much less than adding a special rider to your home or renter's insurance.

Weekly Financial Checklist

Now that you're set up, let's look at the list of chores you need to whiz through on a weekly and monthly basis.

- **Check your account balances.** If your bank offers automated telephone banking, you can call and find out which checks have cleared and what your new balances are. Don't forget to include your ATM cash withdrawals. If you don't have this service through your bank, reconcile your checking account by hand.

- **Examine your credit card receipts.** If your Visa or MasterCard accounts are with your bank, you can review your account via on-line or automated telephone banking. If not, your Visa or MasterCard should have an 800 number that you can call for account balances. Remember that some charges, particularly restaurant tabs and car rentals, may take a few days to show up. Your monthly statement will be the definitive source.

- **Open and review all bills.** Make sure they are accurate, and double-check to see that your last payment was recorded. Make a note of the due date for each bill.

- **Determine which bills need to be paid immediately.** Some people like to pay bills all at once each month, while others prefer to spread them evenly over the course of the month or pay them as they come in. Your choice may depend on how close you are to the hand-to-mouth system of money management.

- **Check to see what large bills are due shortly.** For example, if you pay your car insurance twice a year, you may need to be setting aside money in advance.

Monthly Financial Checklist

On a monthly basis, take a look at this list and confirm that everything is in place. If certain bills, like the rent or mortgage, are due on the first of each month, then run through the monthly checklist by the twenty-fifth (earlier if the mail is particularly slow in your area).

- **Make all non-bill payments.** This includes things like rent, mortgage, car payments, child-care expenses, health insurance, etc.

- **Reconcile all bank statements.** Make sure everything agrees with your records.

- **Review all credit card statements.** Again, make sure all purchase and payment information is accurate. Respond in writing to the credit card company if there is incorrect or missing information and keep copies of all correspondence.

- **Review that month's expenses.** Are you over budget? Under budget? What needs to be adjusted?

- **Review tax issues.** Even if it's May, you need to be planning for next year's taxes, especially if you are self-employed or receive a significant portion of your earnings in cash. You also need to plan ahead if you've received a large sum of money, such as an inheritance or money from a 401(k) that was not rolled over. If you've made a significant charitable contribution, such as donations of clothing or furniture to a church-supported thrift shop, get documentation and keep it with your upcoming tax file.

- **Review investment and retirement plan summaries.** Again, check to see that the information on these statements is accurate and up-to-date.

At this point, you should have your desk and newly reorganized files set up, your scorecard, either electronic or otherwise, in place, and your lists of weekly and monthly chores to run through.

Eight Tips For Money Management Success

By Chris Shipley

Like so many things in life, moving headlong into a personal finance manager, even the best of them, can lead to frustration and end in abandonment of the program. Here are some tips to help you get the most from your program of choice.

1. Start slowly. You don't have to load every last morsel of your financial data into the program at one sitting. An easy way to get started is to begin with your last fully reconciled bank statement. Use the ending balance amount as the beginning balance when you set up your checking and/or savings account. Then enter only the payments and deposits you've made since that statement. Unless you really need to enter a past activity history for budget-building reasons, this is all the foundation you'll ever need.

2. Memorize frequent transactions. Use your software's ability to memorize transaction input so that information such as payee, address, category—and, in certain cases, the amount—will be filled out automatically each time you make repetitive payments. On the other hand, be selective when choosing which transactions your software will memorize and save for recurring use. Too many transactions can actually slow down the check-writing process.

3. Budget carefully. Most programs come with budget categories already set up. Use these as a basis for building your personalized list, creating new categories as you need them. But don't overdo it. Avoid defining budget categories too narrowly. It will take you longer to find the right category as you allocate expenses, and too many categories can yield reports that are less meaningful than those that contain broader categories.

4. Track tax categories. The most useful information you can glean from a checkbook manager may be your deductible expenses. Make sure to establish budget categories for items that are tax deductible, such as medical expenses, mortgage interest, and taxes paid.

5. Record paycheck deductions. Record paychecks as gross deposits, then make payments for your federal and state withholdings, FDIC payments, 401(k) deduction, and so forth. Use the program's memorization and recurring scheduling features to make this easier. Then,

even through your bank statement will only show the net deposit, you'll have a complete, current record of income and withholding for your tax records.

6. Establish a habit for paying bills. Plan to pay all your bills at one or two quick sittings each month. Save up ATM receipts and check-register notations and enter them during one of these sessions. This is much quicker and more convenient than firing up the program each time you incur an expense or make a deposit.

7. Use electronic payment services. If the package you choose links to BillPay or CheckFree, use the service; they save both time and money. First, you can be sure your payment will be received at the merchant when you want it to be, saving late charges. Second, it's faster than addressing, stamping, and licking envelopes.

8. Back up your records to disk. Old news, but it's much more crucial when your personal finances are at stake. If your system goes down or the personal finance manager's data is somehow corrupted, you should not be caught without a disk that reflects your most recent check register and other financial information. With it, you can rebuild your financial picture with little more than aggravation; without it, you're in trouble. Most programs include a backup feature and will remind you to back up data files when you exit the program. Use it.

Used by permission of PC Magazine, January 12, 1993

How To Protect Against A Bad Thing

Anybody who has ever left a well-kept, electronic-gadget-filled home in the morning and come back to an empty house or apartment that night understands why the death penalty remains on the books.

Good record keeping is good protection in case a bad thing happens. Don't rely on your memory to recall what possessions are missing when filling out a police report. Insurance companies base their reimbursement check to you on the report. Put this book down right now and take twenty minutes to put together this burglary/fire-protection package for yourself:

- Make a detailed list of all your valuables. Include clothes, coats, shoes, linens, etc. Remember that a fire or smoke damage can destroy your work wardrobe which, however modest, will be expensive to replace.

- Write down the make, model, and serial numbers of all appliances and electronics. Don't forget things like pagers, computers, and telephones.

- Take pictures of each room in your home and specific shots of high-ticket items, such as artwork, television, and jewelry.

- Make copies of big-ticket receipts.

- Read your renter's or home owner's insurance policy for what exactly is covered and not covered. Also check to see if the insurance company pays full replacement value on a claim.

Keep this package someplace other than your home, either in your safe-deposit box, at the office, or with a family member, and update it regularly. You should also keep your home owner's or renter's insurance current and at a sufficient level to cover replacement of all your valuables at current market prices.

On a personal safety note, if you come home and sense something is wrong when you walk in the door, leave immediately! Call the police from a neighbor's phone. With the exception of your children, dog, or hockey tickets, nothing is worth the potential danger of confronting a felon face-to-face. Besides, you take the chance of mucking up valuable evidence.

CHAPTER 7

The Basics Of Banking

Here's the deal: Banks are like retail stores. Some are similar to national or regional chains and some are like local, mom-and-pop-owned businesses. All have slightly different merchandise, and all charge different prices for similar products.

Banks, like stores, are for-profit businesses. They make money by selling you different financial products and services, like checking accounts, IRAs, and Certificates of Deposit (CDs). Then they use your money to loan out to someone else. They make a profit on the interest paid for borrowing the money. (Credit card companies make money the same way.) All this is legal and above board. The banking industry will never fail the way it did during the Great Depression because it is highly regulated and insured (see FDIC information, on the next page).

Federal Deposit Insurance Corporation (FDIC)

After a wave of banks across the country failed during the Great Depression, the federal government established The Federal Deposit Insurance Corporation, better known as the FDIC. The FDIC guarantees, within limits, funds on deposit in member banks and thrift institutions.

What this means to you is that the days of the local sheriff rounding up a posse to go after the bank robbers are over. Your money (up to $100,000), held in an FDIC-insured bank, is safe from robberies, bank failures, fire, explosions, or any other disaster.

While it's probably harder to find a bank that is not insured by the FDIC, it is worth checking before you open an account. Usually the FDIC sticker is prominently displayed on or near the main doors of a bank, as well as near the teller windows. Ask if you don't see it.

During the past 10 years, some banks, particularly in big cities, have become more discriminating in their acceptance of new customers. Someone who is applying to open an account with a bank, particularly a checking account, may undergo more intense scrutiny than they might have a decade ago. Similarly, a bank may close the account of a customer with a chronic history of bouncing checks. Just as a department store would revoke its own credit card for misuse, so may a bank choose to close the account of a perpetually delinquent customer.

You can guess the reason for the change in bank policy. Too many people did bad things, and banks were left holding the (empty) bag. Remember two things: First, you are the customer, and you deserve consideration and service. Second, banking is a business relationship that is based on trust. You trust the bank to keep your money safe and available to you, and the bank trusts you to not cheat the system.

Finding The Right Bank For You

Forget about the bank that offers a free toaster for opening a new account. (In the end, you're likely to end up paying for that toaster and twelve more like it in higher fees.) There are more critical factors in your choice of banks.

While nothing prevents you from closing your accounts at one bank and moving to another later on, it's really better to find the right institution for you the first time out. Most banks still value loyalty in their customers. A long relationship between you and your bank can be an important factor later on when you go to apply for a loan or a mortgage.

What you are likely to find as you shop for a bank is that there are great similarities in the basic services. If you look at four banks, three may offer nearly identical fees and services, and one, probably the smallest or newest in town, may offer significantly lower fees. If you are just starting out and every penny is critical, the decision of which bank to choose may boil down to straight numbers: Who offers the lowest monthly fees?

At some point down the road, interest rates—both what the bank pays on certain accounts and products, and what you must pay on a loan or mortgage—also will be valuable to you. But initially, the biggest chunk of change at stake is in the monthly fees you pay a bank for its services.

Here is an example of why bank fees are important. Say you opened a savings account with $50 in a bank that paid an exceptionally high 5 percent interest annually. If you never deposited another penny into savings, how much money would you have in one year? Don't bother getting out the calculator. The answer is none. In theory, you should have $52.50 (your original $50, plus $2.50 in interest), but if the bank charges a $7 monthly service fee for any account under $500, that totals $84 a year, which wipes out both your interest and your principle.

The bottom line is pay attention to fees, particularly monthly service fees, bounced check fees, and ATM (automated teller machine) fees. These can add up. (See "The Path Around A Bank's Monthly Service Charges.")

In addition to looking at monthly fees, services charges, and interest rates, here is a list of other bank attributes you may want to consider:

- Location of bank, its branches, and ATMs
- On-line services
- Network ATM affiliation (CIRRUS, NYCE, etc.)
- Mortgage services
- Credit card policies (and interest rates!)

Location was more important before the advent of things like electronic banking, direct deposit, and ATM machines. These days, most problems can be resolved by telephone or modem. However, if your employer does not offer direct deposit, if you live in one state or town and work in another, or if you're in a cash business, location and bank hours may be a higher priority.

The following are handy definitions of the kinds of accounts, products, and services that you'll encounter when shopping for a bank.

Types Of Bank Accounts

Savings Account

A type of account at a bank or savings and loan institution that pays a set amount of interest. As a rule, interest is paid from the first day of deposit to the day of withdrawal. These accounts are also known as statement savings accounts because the depositor receives a monthly summary, or bank statement, that lists the interest earned, the annual percentage yield earned, the rate of interest paid, and any charges incurred.

Passbook Savings Account

This is a savings account where all transactions—deposits, withdrawals, interest payments, etc.—are recorded in a small book kept by the depositor; thus, it requires the depositor to be present in the bank or the book to be mailed in for every transaction. You may have had such an account as a child.

Checking Account

Traditionally, this is a noninterest-bearing, demand-deposit statement account (you get a monthly statement summarizing all activity) from which withdrawals may be made using checks or automated teller machines. Basic checking accounts do not pay interest on the balance. Demand deposit means your funds are available to you at any time.

Most banks offer at least two or three types of checking. Basic checking offers the lowest monthly fee but sometimes limits the number of checks you can write. Usually the first eight or ten checks you write each month are free, and there's a nominal charge (under $1) for every additional check. For the second, mid-level type of checking account, the bank usually charges a flat fee of $10 to $12 per month for an unlimited number of transactions and waives all checking fees for customers with balances of more than $1,000.

No matter what the type of account, you are usually required to order and pay for printed checks. This runs $25 to $50, depending on how many checks you order and how fancy they are. (Uh, just plain checks, please. Find another way to entertain yourself.)

Money Market Account

This interesting financial vehicle is a sort of cross between a checking account and a savings account. It usually requires a larger initial deposit, say $500, that must be maintained, and it puts a strict limit on the number of checks that can be written a month, often from three to six. The advantage of a money market account is that it pays a higher interest rate than a regular savings account. It's a good way to build some serious savings and still have the ability to make withdrawals.

Individual Retirement Account (IRA)

This is an individual account that serves as a personal pension plan. Once you make your initial deposit in an IRA, there is no minimum annual contribution. The maximum annual contribution is $2,000 if the account is held by an individual, $4,000 if held by a two-income couple. The great advantage of an IRA is that the money goes untaxed until you withdraw the funds at retirement, and tax-deferred earnings grow much more quickly than taxable earnings. There are, however, severe penalties if you withdraw early.

Keogh Account

This is an individual pension plan for people who are self-employed or employees of unincorporated businesses. Deposits are limited to 25 percent of annual income up to $30,000 (so do this while you're still poor!). Like IRAs, Keogh Accounts offer significant tax benefits and levy serious penalties if funds are withdrawn early.

Financial Products And Services

Personal Check

A check is a written order directing a bank to pay a specific sum of money to a specific person or organization. It is illegal to write a check if funds have not been deposited to cover the amount of the check. When endorsed (signed on the back) by the payee, a check becomes the equivalent of cash and is considered negotiable.

Automated Teller Machine (ATM)/ATM Card

An ATM is a computerized machine that allows bank customers to use a personal ATM card and secret PIN (personal identification number) to make basic banking transactions, including withdrawing and depositing funds, transferring funds between accounts, checking account balances, and paying bills. ATMs offer the convenience of 24-hour banking. They also allow you to make transactions at any bank, worldwide, that is linked to the same network as your bank—for example, MAC, NYCE, or CIRRUS. For security reasons, there is usually a limit on how much cash can be withdrawn from an ATM each day (usually $500). Some banks charge a fee for ATM transactions, particularly those made at another bank's machine.

Money Order

A money order is a kind of guaranteed personal check. It's purchased from a bank, post office, telephone company, or other financial institution for the amount of the check plus a small fee. Because you have paid up front for the money order, the payee is guaranteed that the check is good. Certain payees, particularly the government, insist on money orders rather than personal checks for just this reason. You can put a stop payment on a money order if you fear that it has been lost or stolen. To lower your risk, make sure you immediately fill in the payee's name when you purchase a money order.

Traveler's Check

These, like money orders, are purchased for their cash value, plus a small issuing fee. Traveler's checks, however, are purchased in specific denominations—$10, $20, $50, $100—from a financial institution like American Express, Visa, MasterCard, most branches of the American Automobile Association (AAA), or a major bank, and they are not made out to a specific payee. Traveler's checks are a safer way to carry your funds than cash because they protect you in case of loss or theft. The first way they do this is by having you sign the checks once in the presence of the issuer and again in the presence of the payee, who then compares the two signatures to prevent forgery. Traveler's checks also come with documentation, similar to a receipt, that assures you that—should they be lost or stolen—you can stop payment and have them reissued at locations nearly everywhere in the world. Make sure you keep the documentation in a separate location than the checks so they are not lost or stolen together!

Safe-Deposit Box

You know this one from the movies. A safe-deposit box is usually a long, slender metal box kept in a vault at the bank. It can be rented as a storage space for valuables—jewelry, deeds, wills, treasure maps, etc. Annual rental fees generally run from $30 to $50, can be paid via mail each year, and are tax deductible. Upon rental of the box, you are given a key. It takes two keys, yours and the banker's, to remove the box from storage. You have the option of granting another person (e.g., spouse, attorney, relative) access to your box upon your death.

Not all banks offer this service. If you are a customer at a small branch, you may have to go to the main bank for a safe-deposit box. Also, not all banks require you to have an account with them to rent a safe-deposit box.

Certificate of Deposit (CD)

This is a deposit that is made with a bank or savings and loan institution for a specific amount of time. This means that you agree to keep the money on deposit, without withdrawal, for a period of anywhere from three months to over five years. The advantage of a CD, in theory, is that it pays a higher interest rate than a savings or money market account. However, there can be a wide range of rates (possibly not as high as those for a money market), and there are severe financial penalties for early withdrawal.

Overdraft Protection Plan

This plan allows you to write a check or checks for up to a certain amount more than what you actually have on deposit. Essentially, the bank offers you, because of your good credit record, something called a "revolving line of credit." Guaranteeing your overdrafts is a way of offering you a preapproved loan. This can be very helpful in an emergency. However, like any loan, the money must be repaid within a predetermined amount of time and usually at a high rate of interest (but less than a bounced-check fee). Use sparingly.

Overdraft protection is dangerous in the same way a credit card is. If you use it to the limit and only make the minimum payment each month, you're throwing a good deal of money away on interest payments.

These are the general products and services most banks offer. In the end, what will matter most to you are the fees, the location of banks and their ATMs, and perhaps what on-line and tele-bank capabilities they offer. Good luck!

The Types Of Banks In America

Commercial Bank

The most familiar type of bank to most of us, these cater to personal and business accounts. They are full-service banks that offer a range of options, from checking and saving accounts to mortgage and car loans, safe-deposit boxes and financial products like IRAs, money market accounts, and retirement and investing planning.

Credit Union

These are not-for-profit financial institutions, usually formed by the employees of a company and operated as a cooperative. They may be very similar to a bank in the services they offer. Credit unions frequently pay higher rates on deposits and charge lower rates on loans than commercial banks.

Savings Bank (a.k.a. Savings & Loan)

Known in the biz as "depository financial institutions," they basically offer savings accounts and home mortgage loans. Scarred by mismanagement in the 1980s, savings banks are now fully insured by the newly created Savings Association Insurance Fund (SAIF), a unit of the FDIC.

Thrift Bank/Thrift Institution

This is an umbrella term for nontraditional banks, such as savings banks, savings and loan banks, and credit unions, that serve primarily as depositories for consumer savings and/or home mortgage loans.

Investment Bank

The terms "investment banks" and "investment bankers" are both misnomers in that they are not traditional banks or bankers. Investment banks are firms, not banks, that give investment advice and buy and sell stocks and bonds on behalf of clients. They may not accept deposits or make loans.

Federal Reserve Bank

Any one of a group of twelve banks that make up the Federal Reserve System. Located in New York, Boston, Richmond, Philadelphia, Atlanta, Chicago, St. Louis, Cleveland, Minneapolis, Kansas City, San Francisco, and Dallas, each bank is owned by the member banks in its region. The function of a Federal Reserve Bank is to monitor the banks in its particular region. The Federal Reserve Bank checks that all commercial and savings banks follow the regulations laid out by the Federal Reserve Board. They act as depositories for member banks in their region and provide emergency funds.

The Path Around A Bank's Monthly Service Charges

Often, the way around your bank's monthly service charge is to maintain—and the operative word here is *maintain*—a minimum balance in your combined accounts. This means if the minimum is $500 and you keep $300 in your savings account and never let your checking balance fall below $200, there are no monthly service fee charges. Bounced or canceled check fees and certain ATM charges may still apply.

However, the moment your combined accounts drop below the minimum balance, even for a day, fees are charged. One of life's great ironies is that in banking, the more money you have, the lower the monthly fees are likely to be.

How To Find The Perfect Bank

Take a couple of lunch hours and visit four or five banks in the area. Lunch time is usually a bank's busiest time, so you can see how well the institution works under pressure. Are there only one or two tellers on duty and a line out the door? Is there a "floater" who answers questions and helps to move things along?

A 20 minute wait for a teller could mean several things. Perhaps half of the staff is out with the flu. Maybe the bank is running a special on CDs. Or maybe it says something about the bank management. On the other hand, if the bank is deserted at lunch time, that is also significant.

Stop by the information or customer service counter and pick up brochures on the services and products you are interested in, including checking and savings accounts, on-line banking, IRAs, credit cards, and bill-paying capabilities. Ask for the current fees, interest rates, and minimum balances if they are not on the brochures.

Go home and review your packages of information in neutral surroundings. In all likelihood, there will be one bank that stands out as having most or all of the services you want, at the right price for you.

Sidestepping ATM Pitfalls

ATMs may be the single greatest banking invention of all time, but they do make it all too easy to withdraw cash without recording your transactions, resulting in an unpleasant, mystery bank balance. Here's what some people do to prevent disaster:

- Always get a receipt, even for a $20 withdrawal. Keep all of the receipts in a safe place and record them in your bank register when you get home.

- Limit yourself to one or two withdrawals a week. This will help your record keeping and your budget.

- When you withdraw cash from an ATM, write out a check for the amount you withdrew and leave it with your checkbook. This will give you a second reminder to record the transaction when you go to reconcile your checking account. It's an expensive trick to play on yourself because checks cost money. However, a few wasted checks are cheaper than one that has bounced.

How To Balance A Checkbook*

To start, you'll need your checkbook register, a calculator, pencil and paper, and your most recent bank statement.

1. Find your closing balance on your bank statement and write it down.

2. Add to this figure any deposits made after the closing date of the statement.

3. Subtract from this new figure any checks that were written after the closing date of the statement.

4. From this new total, subtract any bank fees charged to any of your accounts.

5. Your total should now match the balance in your check register.

If the two figures do not match, redo your math and then the bank's. It is rare that financial institutions make a mistake, but it can happen. If you determine it is the bank's mistake, call or write, explain the problem, and ask for a new, adjusted statement.

---

* If you have Quicken or another software package, the math will be done automatically for you.

CHAPTER 8

Your Most Precious Piece of Plastic

Time for a pop quiz. A credit card is:

A. A financial guardian angel that can save your butt in an emergency

B. A Roto-Rooter machine that rapidly spins you into a deep, dark hole of debt

C. An effective money management tool

D. All of the above.

The correct answer is "D," all of the above. People who misuse credit cards populate the most crowded train currently speeding into personal bankruptcy court. You have a far greater chance of screwing up your financial life for years to come through over-charging on credit cards than you do of catching Lyme disease, and you may be hard-pressed to say which experience is worse.

On the other hand, imagine that you're driving home after spending the holidays with out-of-state relatives when, at 8:30 P.M. on New Year's Eve, your water pump goes out on the West Virginia Turnpike. A valid credit card will probably save your life. (Your AAA membership will be very helpful, too.)

Do not misunderstand. A credit card is a wonderful thing. It enables you to move money around and keep track of what you have spent, in addition to offering considerable security when traveling or in an emergency. The operative word to keep in mind is *respect*. Respect the power of a credit card as if it were a loaded gun. Use it for protection, not sport. It's not just a matter of pissing off the credit card company if you're late on a payment; a boo-boo here will haunt you on your credit report for a minimum of seven years. If you have a credit card, fine. But be vigilant. Make payments on time, put as much as you can toward any outstanding balance, and, please, stay under your credit limit.

How many major credit cards do you need? Listen very carefully to this answer: One. Une. Uno. Make it a major credit card like a Visa or a MasterCard (not American Express) that virtually can be used anywhere and for almost anything. And get one with a credit limit under $1,000. Too much freedom equals too much temptation. Don't double or triple your potential for trouble with multiple credit cards. Unless you have a wealthy parent or Sugar Daddy who is covering the bills, cut up the other major credit cards, pay them off, and slim down to—what's that magic number? One.

Here's the reason why: We all play financial games with ourselves. It's sort of like setting the alarm clock 10 minutes ahead so we don't have to spring out of bed in the morning like a jack-in-the-box. The two-three-four-major-credit-cards game is a dangerous one. You think you're okay because you're "only" carrying $3,000 to $4,000 on each card. You religiously pay the minimum payment each month, on time, and soon those limits are raised to $10,000 or $20,000 per card. You think, "Cool. You never know when you might need $9,000 for an emergency." You take turns paying down the highest card and use the others instead. One day you wake up and you're carrying $80,000 in credit card debt. You're monthly minimum payments—which do almost nothing to reduce the debt—are running you $2,400 a month, and essentially, you're in a financial choke hold.

Don't Play Credit Card Roulette. One Visa or MasterCard will do whatever you need to do (even Lord & Taylor now takes them). One card simplifies your financial life. You will have a better grip on your budget and a better chance of living within your means—a American art lost since the '80s.

Reluctantly, and for credit-building purposes *only*, one or two gas or department store credit cards may be acceptable. Put the department store cards in a bowl of water and freeze them so you won't be tempted to use them casually. If you're married, most couples find it easier for each partner to have a separate credit card.

And finally, a second major credit card is acceptable if you do a considerable amount of traveling and/or entertaining for business and want to keep those business accounts separate from your personal life. (Particularly valuable if you have your own business.) If you routinely run up a couple thousand dollars or more a month for business, ask your company about a corporate credit card where the bill goes straight to your workplace. You'll have to account for the charges, but you won't have to deal with paying another bill.

If you still feel the need for a second card, look into the advantages of a *debit card*. The new debit card offered through banks looks and works just like a Visa or MasterCard. When you use the card, the charges are deducted from your checking account, so essentially, you're paying cash.

If You've Never Had A Credit Card

The truth no one will tell you is that it is possible to live a full and productive life without credit cards. It may require some planning ahead when you travel, but you can survive. From a financial point of view, a credit card is most helpful in building your credit rating. Over a period of time, a credit card shows a record of responsible— or irresponsible—behavior, which is what potential creditors and lending institutions look for before they give out a mortgage or car loan. (More on this in the next chapter.)

Ask yourself this question: Am I the type of person who can walk away from a really great sale or an unbelievably good deal? If you aren't, think very carefully before you sit in on the credit card game. If your budget is tight now, a credit card will make it easier in the short run and hell in the long run. Continue with the Manage-to-Grow Money System and approach the subject again in six months.

The good news here is that there are all kinds of credit cards, and companies are doing back flips to get your business. You are in what will probably always be a favorable buyer's market.

If you've never had a credit card, here's how most work: At the end of the billing cycle, an itemized statement with the total amount you've charged that month comes in the mail. If you pay that total, there is no interest charge. If you make a partial payment, interest is charged on the amount you don't pay off (your outstanding balance). Charging interest is how banks and credit cards make their money.

Your goal, should you choose to accept it, is to find a credit card with the lowest interest rate and no annual fee. Once you find such a card, take good care of it. Remember, too many misuses and some Saturday night you could be standing in line at Blockbuster, about to charge a measly $12 worth of movies, when the cashier calmly takes out a pair of scissors and, right before your eyes, transforms your Most Precious Piece of Plastic into toothpicks.

How To Find The Best Credit Card For You

Americans aren't going to settle for just ten different kinds of breakfast cereal, and they certainly won't tolerate only four or five types of credit cards. There are dozens of different kinds of plastic, maybe even hundreds.

Here are the things to consider when shopping for a credit card:

1. **Annual Fee Or Membership Charge**: If there is a charge, this needs to be factored in with the interest rates.

2. **Annual Percentage Rate (Interest Rate)**: This is the figure you hear so much talk about—the reason being that it can vary dramatically, from 6.5 percent to upward of 21 percent. And it can be a fixed rate or a variable rate, depending on the card you have. Also, some banks offer special "introductory rates" on credit cards to lure you in, then change to a higher rate six months later. Be sure to read the fine print!

   Remember, if you are able to pay off your total every month, there are no finance charges. If you can't pay off your total (and statistics show that about 70 percent of us don't), then you're going to be hit with a finance charge. Essentially, the credit card company is giving you a loan. If you pay off the balance within 30 days, there is no penalty. Otherwise, there is. This is how the company makes money.

   Ideally, you want to pay the lowest interest rate you can find. To help, BankCard Holders of America, (703) 389–5445, or Cardtrack, (800) 344–7714, can send you, for a modest fee, a list of credit card companies with low interest rates and no annual fees.

3. **Balance Subject To Finance Charge For Purchases**: Banks or credit card companies can assess the finance charge, which is based on the interest rate, in several ways. How they assess it—daily, monthly, yearly—affects how much you must pay. The most advantageous way for you is to have new purchases assessed daily and that sum added to your running balance. For instance, say you don't use your credit card at all until the third week of your cycle. You don't want to have to pay a full month's interest on that purchase. Check the math!

4. **Grace Period For Repayment Of Balances**: For new purchases, you generally have between 20 and 32 days (depending on your billing cycle) to pay off the balance before finance charges are added. On your bill, it will say, "Payment Due Date." After that date, finance charges will be added.

   Keep in mind that for cash advances on your credit card, there often is no grace period. A second deterrent is that the finance charge is far greater than it is with purchases. If you're doing this on a regular basis, quit. It's costing more than it's worth. Use your ATM card.

You will have to shop around for the best rate on credit cards. Many banks list their rates in their windows so you don't even have to go in. Often the lowest rates are available only to people with Gold Card credit ratings. Also, be aware that a really good rate may include an annual fee, which can erase the benefit.

If you already have a credit card and you're satisfied with the level of service, call to see if you can negotiate a lower rate. Threaten to cancel your card (and be prepared to, if you must). A credit card company may not be able to match what you're demanding, but credit card officials often will lower it.

Now, if you really want to buck the system, find a no-fee, lowest-interest-rate-in-town credit card and pay off the balance within the grace period. Nobody will make a dime off you.

Your Precious Piece Of Plastic Procedure

We all know that few things send you off for a prolonged visit in Debt City more often than the misuse of credit cards. You know the wrong way to use a credit card; here's what financial planner Ray Martin suggests:

Every time you use your credit card, deduct the amount from your checkbook (as if you've paid cash). Purchase a blouse at Macy's's for $53.22? Subtract it from your checking balance. New golf balls at the pro shop? Take that $18.90 off your checkbook. Then at the end of the month when the bill comes in, voila! You have the money to pay the account in full. You'll never pay interest or late charges on your credit card again.

CHAPTER $9

How To Build, Protect, And, If Necessary, Restore Your Credit

What exactly is credit? The prestigious financial firm of Dun & Bradstreet defines credit in the company's motto as "man's confidence in man." You, however, may remember being introduced to this enormously appealing concept at a tender age via the Popeye cartoon character Wimpy. He summarized the concept of credit in his best-known line, "I'll gladly pay you Tuesday for a hamburger today."

As far as it can be determined, we probably have farmers to thank for the modern concept of credit. The buy-now-pay-later system was developed to tide them over between "paychecks" when their crops were harvested and sold at market. Not surprisingly, the concept of credit has flourished over the years and today we are flooded with more credit granted than ever before.

Trouble arises when we recognize the fun but not the responsibility that comes with credit. Essentially, credit enables you to borrow money against your good name with the promise that you will pay it back. Sometimes *collateral* (resalable property or merchandise that you already own) is required; almost always a check that you are a person of your word is performed before credit is extended. Here's the bottom line: Used wisely, credit can (1) save your butt in an emergency and (2) help you to build wealth. Misuse credit and it can bury you.

In this chapter, we will address how to build credit, protect it, and, if necessary, repair it. However, before we go any further, consider this: Credit requires a medium-to-high level of discipline. If you feel you're not at that level yet, if your spending reflexes still routinely out-muscle your saving resolve, there is no dishonor in sticking with the pay-as-you-go route. On the other hand, if you think you are ready to test yourself as a financially responsible adult, here's what you need to know.

How To Establish Credit

The truth is you could live a rich and full life without the benefits of credit. Most people did for the first three quarters of this century. If you rarely travel and you anticipate inheriting your family home, you might choose to pass altogether on the temptation credit offers.

Credit serves three really useful purposes. It enables you to make large purchases, like a car, refrigerator, or house, by borrowing the money and paying it back over a period of time. (If most of us had to wait until we'd saved $122,000—the median price of a house today—in cash to purchase a home, our children would be pushing 40.) Second, credit helps in many kinds of emergencies, ranging from needing a new transmission for your car to loss of your job. And third, for the sophisticated money manager, credit can be used to build wealth. (More examples of this later.)

Credit Rating

This is a formal evaluation of an individual's credit history and capability of repaying financial obligations. (In English, it's a report card on how well you pay your bills on time.)

The key is to use credit as if it were cayenne pepper, not sugar. So, if you feel you're ready, proceed.

The Scorekeeper: Your Credit Report

The first thing to understand is that credit is not an inalienable right. Likewise, a good credit rating, which everyone needs before they can get credit, is not something you're born with. Each of us must prove our credit worthiness over a period of time before we're given credit. It's one of those catch-22's in life, similar to getting your first job. You need experience to get a job, and to get experience, you need a job. Annoying, isn't it? Obviously, millions of people resolve this catch-22. Here's what you need to know.

A credit rating is literally a score assigned to you by credit bureaus like Experian (formerly called TRW). Credit bureaus investigate, analyze, and maintain records on the credit responsibility of an individual (Dun & Bradstreet does the same for companies) and then assign a numerical score based on your age, employment record, income, and history of repaying debt. This score becomes part of your overall credit report.

A creditor, the person or company giving you credit, is allowed to establish its own rules for extending credit as long as the guidelines are not discriminatory (e.g. redheads only) and are within federal regulations. Among the acceptable reasons for credit denial are insufficient credit references, temporary or irregular employment and/or residence, insufficient income, and no credit rating or a delinquent credit rating.

Sound serious? It is. Every time you apply for a job, a loan, an apartment, a mortgage, or a credit card, people can call up your credit report to see if you are a law-abiding citizen. You can hide the fact that you flunked chemistry far easier than you can hide those five delinquent car payments.

Remember the Get-12-CDs-Free offer that also required you to purchase another twelve CDs within a year? You may have blown it off, but the credit report company did not. Any financial obligation you fail to meet is usually reported to the credit company and *it stays on your record for seven years* or until you resolve it. Even if the delinquent bill is paid, it may still remain on your record.

Diana Nichols is a twenty-something credit repair expert and director of Gold Key Credit Services in Westchester, New York. She says people often are unaware that they have a credit problem until they go to make a major purchase, like a house or a car, and are turned down by the mortgage or loan officer. "It's devastating because their dream must be put on hold until the credit problems are resolved. That may take a couple of weeks or it may take years, depending on the extent of the problems," says Diana.

Trying to repair your credit rating is much like root canal work —it's long, tedious, costs a lot, and is certainly uncomfortable. "The idea is to not go there in the first place," she says. We will talk about how to fix bad credit later; here are her suggestions on how to build a good credit rating from scratch.

Credit Scoring

Things that increase your credit score:
Home phone
Bank credit card
Checking and savings accounts
Professional job
Membership in labor union
Over fifty years of age
More than fifteen years on the job

Things that subtract from your credit score:
Debt
Delinquency
Less than five years on the job

Diana's Four Rules For Building A Sparkling Credit Rating

1. Determine the facts.

You may already have a credit history and not know it. Call or write at least two of the credit bureaus to see if they have a credit report on you. Most of the credit bureaus will send you one free copy of your credit report a year. Otherwise, it costs from $8 to $15 a copy. Obtain a credit report, then check to make sure the information is correct. If it's not, you can correct it by writing the credit report company directly.

"You cannot hide," says Diana. "When you do a good or bad thing, it will be on the report. However, there can be incorrect information. If there are people that have the same name as you, like Mike Davis, or if you're a junior and your father's a senior, information can get mixed up."

Also, keep in mind that credit bureaus don't automatically remove the report of a problem that has been resolved. Double-check that this has been done immediately. "When you're negotiating with the creditor or collection agency on the final payment of an account, include this issue. What you want is the entire dispute removed from your record, not just a note that it has been resolved. Get it in writing that this will be done upon payment."

2. Build a nest egg.

Few things impress a potential lender like money in the bank. And, not incidentally, it goes a long way toward protecting you from damaging your credit rating. Diana recommends that you "save until you have three months of expenses in the bank."

3. Open different types of credit accounts.

This is very hard advice for us to pass on since we just lobbied *hard* in the last chapter to severely limit the temptation of numerous credit cards. However, Diana is correct. Initially, to establish your credit worthiness, it is valuable to have three, maybe four accounts— a gas card, department store card, Visa or MasterCard—and pay off the balances regularly.

Understand that this is a financial exercise with one goal: To establish that you are an honorable adult who settles his or her financial obligations promptly. This is not a license to open an account at every department store in town and run up the balance to its limit. Make whoopee on New Year's, not on your credit report.

Here's a good rule of thumb for the financially challenged (you know who you are): *Never charge anything that can be worn or eaten.* Pay cash and if you don't have the money, don't buy it.

4. Get a secured credit card.

If you have had credit problems in the past or if you have no credit rating (which can be just as limiting), consider taking out a secured Visa or MasterCard. The way a secured card works is you put down a deposit, usually between $200 and $500, and you are issued a credit card with a low limit—often whatever the deposit is. The Visa or MasterCard works just like a credit card, only with your deposit held as collateral. By the way, no one can tell by looking that it is a secured card.

Once you have established that you can pay the bills on time (usually twelve months), the deposit is returned to you with interest. Consider opening a secured card account at your bank where you can make a payment, either at an ATM or over the phone, simply by transferring funds directly from your checking account.

It also enables you to check your available credit on the card at any time.

Secured Credit Cards

Marine Midland National
Credit Group
P.O. Box 1351
Buffalo, NY 14240
(800) 874–2100

Chevy Chase Bank
P.O. Box 999
Frederick, MD 21705
(800) 937–5000

Capital One Bank
P.O. Box 85018
Richmond, VA 23285
(800) 333–7116

How To Protect Your Credit

The best way to safeguard your good credit rating—apart from paying bills on time—is to routinely obtain a copy of your credit report to verify that all information is correct.

Pick a date, say your birthday, anniversary, or April 15th (tax day) and every year on that day call and order a credit report from one of the major bureaus. Check to make sure that all the information is current and correct.

Collection agencies can be quick to take your money and slow to remove a "misunderstanding" from your record. This is why it is vital to keep canceled checks and all correspondence from any problem you have. If there is a problem, write to the credit bureau and include copies (never the originals) with your letter.

The credit bureau will let you know if your documentation is acceptable. If not, you must go back to the original creditor or collection agency to enlist help in correcting the inaccuracy. Be relentless in your letter-writing campaign. After all, what's the point of settling a problem if it still haunts you?

Not all problems on a credit report are the result of ignored bills. People can have a legitimate complaint against a creditor (the bill is incorrect, merchandise was damaged or never received, etc.) and the claim is sent into collection while they're trying to resolve it. Most banks, mortgage companies, loan officers, and such will take this into consideration if you have an otherwise clean report.

However, a more vital issue to be aware of as you review your credit report each year is outright criminal fraud. With little more than your name and social security number, a thief can open an account (department and electronics stores are particularly easy), then run up a fortune in charges before the scam is uncovered. In most cases, you are not financially responsible for fraudulent charges, but the delinquency can show up on your credit report.

Always be very careful about giving out your social security number, credit card numbers, or any other personal financial information either over the phone or over the Internet on an unsecured browser. And, of course, there is no legitimate reason for giving anyone your PIN (with the possible exception of your spouse).

How To Repair Your Credit

Doctors, lawyers, movie stars, Olympic athletes, even astronauts can have serious, crippling credit problems. No one is immune. It happens. Here's how to fix it.

1. Get a copy of your credit report.

As credit expert Diana Nichols says, "Most people don't realize they have a problem until they are turned down for credit. If you apply for a credit card, loan, or mortgage and are turned down, the financial institution is required by law to send you, in writing, the reason your application was denied."

The first thing to do is get a copy of your credit report. In terms of difficulty, the report itself is on par with a multi-account bank statement. You have to read it carefully, line by line, to understand exactly what it says.

2. Check the report for errors.

The problem could be an incorrect social security number, name, or address. The Fair Credit Reporting Act requires that all errors be corrected promptly. If the problem is a case of mistaken identity (a misspelled name, incorrect social security number), a letter to the credit bureau with the correct information should clear your report. However, if the error was made by the creditor (you made a payment that was not recorded, you never had an account with them, etc.), the mistake can only be rectified by the creditor.

Send a letter to the creditor stating that you are writing under the provisions of the Fair Credit Billing Act to ask for immediate correction of the error on your credit report. Explain the inaccuracy and ask for written confirmation that the correction was made. By law, the creditor has ninety days to do this.

On the other hand, if the problems are legitimate, here's the drill for correcting the situation and restoring your good credit rating.

3. Communicate with your creditors.

"The thing that makes creditors the maddest is to be ignored," says Diana. "Chances are, they have communicated with you about an unpaid bill repeatedly and over a long period of time before, as a last resort, they send a delinquent account to a collection agency. *The moment it goes to a collection agency, it is on your credit report for seven years!*"

"What you should understand is that it is not in the creditor's best interest to send an account to a collection agency because the agency gets a significant cut of whatever is recovered. The original creditor never gets anywhere near the full amount owed," Diana explains. "Likewise, it's not in your best interest to have your account go to the collection agency because then, whatever happens—even if you pay off the debt in full the next day—it's a black mark on your credit report."

Diana says that the vast majority of creditors will work with you to establish a payment plan you can live with. "Some may even settle for less than the amount owed. Nearly everyone would rather try to get most of the money back over a longer period of time than nothing at all . . . As hard as it is, it's far better to call and calmly try to work something out—even repayment of $5 a week—than to ignore the situation. It will not go away and can only get worse."

The first step is to call each creditor and say that you want to work out a resolution on the account. Be straightforward and businesslike. You do not owe anybody a reason or an excuse, and they don't want to hear it.

If the debt is more than a year old, some creditors will settle for an amount of money that is less than what you actually owe. For instance, say you ran up a $2,000 bill on your QVC credit account two years ago. The collection agency now handling the account may offer two possibilities: Either a straight settlement of the account with a payment of $1,200 today or three payments of $500 over the next three months. This may or may not be within your financial ability. Negotiate with the agency until you can work out a payment plan. The sooner you pay it off, the quicker your credit report is cleared.

4. Negotiate with creditors for removal of a delinquency from your credit report.

Creditors have the option of either reporting that the credit problem was resolved or removing it from your file completely.

5. Revamp your budget to pay off debts.

You didn't think this was going to be painless, did you? Sit down, take a look at your budget, and see how fast you can pay off this debt.

6. Check after ninety days to see that your credit report is accurate.

If your credit problems have been caused by a major personal catastrophe—a lost job, illness or death in the family, business failure— you do have the option of submitting a short paragraph of explanation to appear on your credit report. However, Diana advises against including divorce in this statement since there is evidence that divorced people are still discriminated against by potential creditors, even though the law prohibits it.

Student Loans

Credit expert Diana Nichols says that if you are having serious problems meeting your student loan payments, speak with the loan officer. In most cases, you can arrange to reduce the payments to a manageable rate or even apply for a temporary deferment— sometimes as long as a year. Check with your loan company for details.

CHAPTER 10

How To Grow Money

Ready for dessert? Good. If you have been a good rookie and accomplished Step 1, covering your living expenses, and you're closing in on Step 2, building a nest egg, then it's time to start thinking about Step 3, using your money to make more money through investments. This final segment of the Manage-to-Grow Money System is where the real fun begins!

You already suspect that investing, because it involves money, can be a fairly emotional activity for some folks. A considerable number of otherwise intelligent people in this country shy away from investing. Some remember the enormous devastation inflicted by the stock market crash of 1929. Others harbor a general contempt for all financial institutions, even banks. But many people simply don't want to get involved in a game they don't understand.

Granted, investing is the chess game of money. It is both an art and a science. Investing carries its own language, which some find debilitating. It's not, and we'll show you how to start off gently.

This chapter is divided into two parts. First, we'll run over the general things you need to keep in mind before you invest that first penny. Then we will focus on the more specific information you'll need in order to march right into a discount brokerage firm and make your first investment decision.

Finally, keep in mind that everything there is to know about investing cannot be summarized in one chapter. The basics are here, but you will learn a great deal more about the investment process as you go about making your first investment. While we are on the subject, run down the list of investing terms in the "Encyclopedia of Financial Terms." This will help get your brain accustomed to the special language used in investing.

First, though, let's talk about what investing is and why growing money isn't just fun, it's necessary.

Why Invest?

Why is investing such a vital part of effective money management? Well, here's what I didn't mention in the chapter on saving because it's a little depressing: Over the long haul, just saving money in a low-interest savings account doesn't cut it. Why? Inflation! A dollar put away today may only be 41 cents thirty years from now.

Bummer, huh? If you are saving for something big, like a house, college tuition for your kids, or retirement, what you want is the dollar you save today to be worth a dollar when you need it in a few years. Don't throw in the towel yet. There are two solutions. You can either (1) save up what you think you'll need plus a third more to cover the cost of inflation or (2) invest your money to generate interest that will make up for the damage of inflation (and then some). Think about it while you make a cup of tea.

The Ravages Of Inflation

Do you remember what you paid for a candy bar, a magazine, or a ticket to the movies when you were a kid? What do you pay now? The cost of things goes up. It's called inflation, and while it can slow down, or even level off, nobody has ever seen inflation hit full reverse throttle.

Over time, the value of a dollar can erode faster than beachfront property. If you don't put most of your savings into the long-term investments that grow through the interest earned, inflation will make the money worth less than its original value. Remember, inflation, not setbacks in the stock market, will do the most damage to your money.

Here's an example that hurts. If inflation rises at an annual rate of about 4 percent, an uninvested $40,000 nest egg today will be worth less than $8,000 in 40 years. What to do? Invest your money so it will grow faster than the rate of inflation.

Keep these things in mind when contemplating an investment in the stock market: While investing in stock is not synonymous with gambling, it is not without significant risk. However, patience is a key instrument in softening that risk.

Then And Now: How Inflation Grows

This is why people on a fixed income are hurt by inflation and why you'll be hurting if you don't set up an investment plan that adds more to your money than inflation takes away.

1967		1997
10 cents	candy bar	75 cents
22 cents	bread	$1.55
$3,310	automobile	$11,700
5 cents	stamp	32 cents
10 cents	newspaper	50 cents
57 cents	half gallon of milk	$1.47
33 cents	gallon of gas	$1.42
$2	movie ticket	$8

Everyone Is An Expert

Here are a couple of encouraging thoughts about how to choose stock investments. Peter Lynch, the legendary Wall Street expert, wrote in his best-selling book, *One Up On Wall Street*, that "any normal person using the customary three percent of the brain can pick stocks just as well, if not better, than the average Wall Street expert . . . . If you stay half-alert, you can pick the spectacular performers right from your place of business or out of the neighborhood shopping mall, and long before Wall Street discovers them."

The Beardstown Ladies did exactly that. Their women-only investment club tends to pick (after extensive research) the stocks of companies whose products they relate to. It works. The club enjoys

The Rule of 72

You can figure out how long it will take an investment to double by using something called the rule of 72. This is how it works: Divide 72 by the interest rate to get the number of years it will take to double your money. For example, $1,000 invested at 9% interest will grow to $2,000 in eight years.

You can also use the rule of 72 to figure out how fast prices will double due to inflation. If you take the current inflation rate, say it's 4.3%, and divide it into 72, it equals 16.7. This means that in just under 17 years a car that now sells for $33,000 will cost $66,000; two tickets to the movies will run $32; and a Little Caesar's pizza will be $19.98.

an average annual return of 23.4 percent. The revered stock market investor Warren Buffett "only" has an average annual return of 23 percent.

In her *Wall Street Journal* column "Your Money Matters," Georgette Jasen writes regularly about "The Experts Versus the Dartboard," an interesting study on picking stocks. First, a stock portfolio is compiled by flinging darts at the stock tables. Then, a panel of six nationally renowned financial experts (the cast changes every six months) pick their own group of stocks and pit it against the dartboard group. Every six months, Ms. Jasen checks in to see which imaginary portfolio is earning more.

So guess who's winning? Lately, the dartboard has been doing very well, sometimes returning as much as 11.5 percent, compared to the experts' 2 percent. However, after analyzing the portfolios' overall performances since the contest began in 1990, Ms. Jasen reports that the pros are "comfortably ahead of both the darts and the industrial average."

Now don't run screaming from the room. You're not going to have to throw anything to start investing in the stock market. If it seems to you that the stock market is getting more attention here as a potential investment vehicle, you're right. The reason is that most other investment opportunities—bonds, T-bills, CDs—are fairly straightforward. You invest the money, and in X amount of time, you receive the money back with X amount of interest. No such guarantees with stock.

So let's begin with a few brief pointers on beginning investment. Here is some expert advice from Ray :

Ray Martin's Eight Rules For Freshmen Investors

1. Start early.

Time is an enormous advantage because of the magic of compound interest. If you save $3 a day ($1,095 a year) for twenty-five years and invest it so that it earns 9 percent compound interest, you should end up with $100,000! The clincher is that less than $30,000 will be money you actually contribute, the rest is the result of compound interest. It does most of the work for you. (See compound interest chart on p. 45.)

2. Only invest money you won't need to live on.

This means you can't use the money that should go toward your monthly expenses or your nest egg. If you do, playing the stock market becomes gambling.

Can You Handle The Risks?

Before making any new investment, ask yourself the following questions:

- Do you understand the potential risks as well as the rewards?
- Have you diversified your investments so all don't carry the same kind—or degree—of risk?
- Do you know how to check your investment performance? Are you committed to doing so at least once a month?
- Do you understand it well enough to explain it clearly to someone else?
- Have you not chosen this investment because someone else talked you into it?
- Do you know the worst one-year loss it has suffered in the past 10 years? Could you tolerate such a loss?
- Will you be able to sleep at night if this investment experiences the normal ups and downs of the stock market?
- Does everything about this deal make sense to you?

If you can't answer "yes" to most—and preferably all—of these questions, you should probably reconsider.

From "Are You Playing It Too Safe With Your Money?" by Gordon Williams. Used with permission of Women's Day magazine, 10.12.93.

---

3. Start slow.

Don't sit in on a poker game that's way over your head. Do your homework. Read. Catch the financial shows on TV. Talk to experts and friends. Then set your investment goals. Learn to drive on a couple of mutual funds (a diversified financial instrument where someone else does the heavy lifting for you), then cautiously add a few racier stocks for the thrill of a quick return (or loss). Remember, if it sounds too good to be true, it is.

4. Disregard the "Buy Low/Sell High" strategy.

There are maybe four people in the entire continental United States who "play the market" and know when it has reached its low point for buying and its high point for selling. You're not one of them. If you're looking for a money sport, try the Kentucky Derby on the first weekend in May (and don't bet the favorite).

5. Reduce risk by diversifying.

Diversifying means not putting all your eggs in one basket or, in this case, spreading out the risk by participating in several different kinds of investments. As a twenty-something investor, you have time to take risks. However, that doesn't mean you should play stock market roulette. If you diversify your portfolio and hold on to your stocks long enough, the risk of investing falls to near zero.

6. Reinvest all profits.

If you cash out and take a trip to Europe every time your mutual fund pays a pretty dividend, count on sitting by a kerosene-burning space heater when you're sixty-seven.

7. Keep your eye on the ball, but don't obsess.

Checking your stock or mutual fund every day can shake your confidence because benefits only come over the long term. Glance at your portfolio weekly, study it quarterly, make decisions semiannually.

8. Investing is not gambling.

At the risk of contradicting your Great Aunt Edna, the stock market is not a casino. In Las Vegas, no matter what game you play, the house eventually wins, and the longer you play, the more the odds go against you. When you're an investor, particularly a twenty-something investor, the opposite is true: The longer you're in, the more you will win.

Those are the ground rules. Here's the next step. . .

Let's Go Shopping

Okay, we're on the launch pad counting down. Run down the checklist:

- Your nest egg is safely socked away.
- You have $1,000 available to dip your toe into the investing pool.
- You understand the risks and benefits, and have answered "yes" to most of the questions in the "Can You Handle The Risks?" quiz.

Good. Now let's make up a grocery list of the kinds of investments you might be interested in. It's a big store and the product line runs from America Online stock to zero coupon municipal bonds. Here's what you need to know to make your decision:

Fixed-Income Investments

Ray says that there are basically two sides to the investment coin: You can be a *loaner*, where you lend money to a bank, company, or the government, or you can become an *owner*, where you purchase a piece of a company (a share of stock). Most investors eventually end up doing both, but for very different reasons. You, on the other hand, do not have to start out ambidextrous. We'll explain both strategies and your options.

There are three good reasons for becoming just a loaner. They are (1) if you are simply too terrified to handle loss of any kind, even short-term loss, (2) if the ups and downs of the stock market make you howl at the moon, or (3) if you're financially comfortable and merely want to protect the wealth you have from inflation.

As a loaner, you might invest in something, like a corporate bond, that is a fixed-income investment. Investors buy bonds in return for regular interest payments. When the bond matures, the issuer pays back the original principal (or the amount of the original investment) to you, the bondholder. This is a

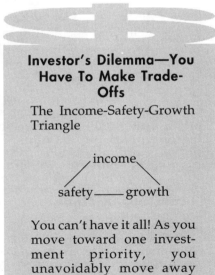

Investor's Dilemma—You Have To Make Trade-Offs

The Income-Safety-Growth Triangle

income
safety —— growth

You can't have it all! As you move toward one investment priority, you unavoidably move away from another.

safe investment because you know what you're putting in, what you'll get back, and the precise time frame for it to happen. But it is not risk-free. Changes in interest rates, particularly rising interest rates, affect bonds and your ability to sell them later because they have to compete with new bonds on the market. The biggest risk, however rare, is if the government agency or company issuing the bonds goes bankrupt. This is why it is vital to buy bonds that carry a high rating by a reputable bond-rating service. (See "Encyclopedia of Financial Terms" for more details.)

Other examples of fixed-income investments are Certificates of Deposit (CDs), U.S. Savings Bonds, U.S. Treasury securities, municipal bonds, and cash-equivalent securities with maturities of under one year. Remember, for all of these, your money is tied up and there are significant penalties for pulling it out early.

Here are Ray's tips for buying fixed-income securities:

- Use a money market fund instead of a bank savings account. Money market funds are typically available at banks or brokerage firms (but your best rates are at a brokerage firm rather than a bank because it cuts out the middleman).

- Buy only the highest rated (triple or double A) corporate or municipal bonds.

- Buy Treasury securities backed by the full faith and credit of the U.S. government.

- Shop around for the best deal on CDs. Banks and brokers sell CDs, and there can be a significant difference in the interest rate each pays. Also, make sure the CDs you purchase are insured by the FDIC.

- Here's the double-edged sword: The longer the maturity of a bond, the higher the rate you get paid. On the other hand, the longer the maturity, the longer you are susceptible to losing value due to rising interest rates.

- There are no free rides. As a rule, the higher the yield on a fixed-rate income investment, the higher the risk.

Investing In Stock

To play the *owner* side of the investment coin means to purchase a piece, or share, of a company. Ray says that stock represents real ownership in a business and participation in the company's future. "You're saying, 'I have faith that, over the long term, business will continue to grow and make money.' If you can make that statement, then by all means invest in stocks."

Keep in mind when you invest in the ownership of a company by purchasing stock, you are not guaranteed any interest or even protection of your principal. Understanding that, here are the two ways you make money:

- If the company increases in value or if ownership in the company is in great demand, the prices of its shares go up.

- If your company has excess profits it pays a portion of them as dividends to the stockholders. Stocks of large, well-established companies usually pay larger, more regular dividends than stocks of smaller or younger companies.

Here's the deal: To really minimize your risk (and enjoy the benefits) of investing in stock, you have to go long term. For instance, if someone invested $1,000 in a diversified group of common stocks in 1947, left the principal alone and reinvested the dividends, that original $1,000 investment would be worth about $360,000 today! On the other hand, if that same person had gone the really safe route and bought Treasury bonds, they now would have $17,500. Big difference, huh?

The message we learn from history is that the longer the time frame, the narrower the range of average returns and the greater the likelihood of positive, attractive returns. For instance, if you look at one-year increments for the time period from 1960 to 1996, common stocks gained as much as 52.6 percent or lost as much as 26.5 percent. But if you take the average returns for five or ten year periods, the range of returns narrows. Take a look at these numbers over the years:

THE STOCK MARKET'S UPS AND DOWNS

Year:	Rate of Return:	Year:	Rate of Return:
1960	0.5%	1979	18.4%
1961	26.9%	1980	32.4%
1962	–8.7%	1981	–4.9%
1963	22.8%	1982	21.4%
1964	16.5%	1983	22.5%
1965	12.5%	1984	6.3%
1966	–10.1%	1985	32.2%
1967	23.9%	1986	18.5%
1968	11.1%	1987	5.2%
1969	–8.5%	1988	16.8%
1970	4.0%	1989	31.5%
1971	14.3%	1990	–3.2%
1972	18.9%	1991	30.5%
1973	–14.7%	1992	7.7%
1974	–26.5%	1993	10.0%
1975	37.2%	1994	1.3%
1976	23.8%	1995	37.4%
1977	–7.2%	1996	23.1%
1978	6.6%		

Here's what the stock market did over a 36-year period. Notice that in 1994 there was only a 1.3 percent increase. And in 1981 and 1990, both recession years, the market was down 4.9 percent and 3.2 percent. But look at what happened during most of the 1980s and 1990s. Sometimes the market was up 30 percent or more. No CD in the world pays that.

Here's an example that you may vaguely remember. In 1987, the stock market dropped nearly 1,000 points in less than three months. It wasn't pretty. If you had invested money at the beginning of that period hoping to sell a few months later, you would have lost your shirt. However, if you had hung on for two years, you would have recovered your money and then some! See? It's not a boring game.

Getting Wet

For your maiden voyage into the unpredictable seas of investing, we strongly recommend starting with a mutual fund. Take a minute and read the full definition in the "Encyclopedia of Financial Terms" now. Basically, a mutual fund is an investment vehicle that puts money in several different places such as stocks, bonds, options, futures, currencies, or money market securities. The appealing advantage is that your money is diversified and managed by a professional. On any given day, there are probably more than 8,000 mutual funds to choose from.

Ready? Here's the step-by-step drill:

1. Open an account with a discount investment firm.

Locate a Fidelity or Charles Schwab office near you. Go in and tell the representative that you would like information on mutual funds (they'll give you two or three pounds of stuff) and an application to open an account. Don't stay, bring it all home.

This next decision is important: If you are only going to buy one mutual fund to start, forget Fidelity or Schwab and go straight to the mutual fund you want (see next section on how to find one).

2. Find a mutual fund that you like.

Between the Fidelity/Schwab material and any recent issue of *Money* magazine, you can find a couple of funds you like. There should be an 800-number listed with the fund. Call to find out what the minimum initial investment is. There is a significant group of mutual funds that starts in the $500 to $1,000 range. There are also some that can run as high as $100,000 (stay away from these your first time out). Choose a $1,000 fund or, better yet, two at $500 (then you can compare how each does).

3. Send in your check and application.

Or take it back into Fidelity or Schwab personally. It will take two to three weeks to be set up.

4. Watch what happens.

Shortly, your monthly statements will start rolling in. Your investment may go up or it may go down. Stay cool. Remember, it's not the month-to-month you're interested in, it's the long-term numbers—like over ten years—that matter. Reinvest your earnings (your broker can tell you how to do this). It will increase your investments significantly.

We think you will find this fun and maybe even mildly addictive. If you're ready to make a bold move, look at your budget. Is there an extra $50 or $100 a month you feel you can comfortably afford to invest? Consider setting up an automatic deduction plan with Fidelity or Schwab (or your mutual fund) and your bank. Then, each month, the amount you designated will automatically be deducted from your account. It can start an impressive roll!

How Dollar-Cost Averaging Reduces Your Risk

Here's how dollar-cost averaging works: Suppose you take $100 a month and invest for a five-month period in a stock mutual fund. Let's say the fund sells for $10 in the first month, $5 in the second, $2.50 in the third, $5 in the fourth, and $10 in the fifth month. You would own 100 shares after five months! With the fund selling at $10 a share, your investment is worth $1,000. Had you bought all your shares during the first month, you could have afforded only 50 shares and would not have made a cent over the five months. Here is how it plays out:

Month	Investment	Share Price	No. of Shares
1	$100	$10.00	10
2	$100	$5.00	20
3	$100	$2.50	40
4	$100	$5.00	20
5	$100	$10.00	10
Total	$500	$10.00	100

Good. Now let's move on to the next chapter, where we talk about money and sex. We know you've been anxiously waiting for this.

CHAPTER 11

Money and Dating: Who Pays?

If you thought budgeting was tricky, saving money a challenge, and investing a mind-blowing experience, hold on to your pockets. In this chapter, we address the single most disruptive issue any two people in love (or in like) have to face, and no, it's not birth control.

Why devote a whole chapter to money and couples? Money, in case you haven't noticed, is a highly emotional subject. (Remember Golden Rule No. 2, "Emotion Is The Enemy"?) At this point, hopefully, getting your own finances set up and properly organized has helped you to eliminate, or at least recognize, certain counterproductive behaviors. Not an easy accomplishment. Now, are you ready to manage money in tandem with another person?

A couple of very unhappy facts of life are that one in every two marriages ends in divorce and that conflict over money is the most frequently cited reason for a breakup. This gives merit to casting at least a casual eye toward how a significant other handles money. As our relationship expert says, most people can handle any previously known personality flaw in their mate, it's the surprises that do couples in.

If you're single in the late 1990s and dating, the issue of money is likely to come up early in a fledgling relationship, and it will continue to come up for as long as you are a couple. Specifically, "Who pays?" for the date is the single hardest question any couple has had to face since God asked Adam and Eve who bit into the apple. Forty years ago, the million-dollar query was "Should you kiss on a first date?" Twenty years ago, it got juicier: "Do you have sex on the first date?" Those puzzles may still be around, but they've taken a back seat (ha ha) to the big one: "Who pays?" It is a question that will plague many couples for as long as they live, or until the ink is dry on the divorce decree, whichever comes first.

From a strictly financial point of view, what has changed on the American social scene is that the "Equal Pay For Equal Work" thing started in the 1970s is now becoming a reality. The majority of women in this country work, and their salaries are beginning to gain parity with men's. This is a good thing and it goes a long way toward eliminating the centuries-old man-pays-for-everything rule.

So, what are the new rules for "Who pays?" The indication from the Class of 2003 is that we're rapidly becoming a Dutch treat society. Many high school students have some sort of part-time job, and both sexes seem perfectly at ease discussing who pays for what. Particularly with high-ticket events such as homecoming dances, proms, and graduation night where limos and expensive dinners may be required, the growing majority of these modern couples candidly divvy up expenses.

This is a perfectly equitable practice, but it poses a problem for the 122 million of us caught between the man-pays-for-everything and Dutch treat generations. It's hard to know who is, or isn't, locked into the traditional mind-set of the man as sole financial provider.

What to do? Here are some interesting pointers from Magda Polenz, M.D., a Manhattan psychiatrist who specializes in couples and relationships. Let's start with the moment of couple conception.

The First Date

The universally held position is that when Person A asks Person B out on a first date, Person A pays. At this particular moment in our evolution, the gentleman still does most of the asking. However, it is not unheard of these days for the lady to make the first move. (Haven't you been reading *Cosmo*?)

How can you be sure who's paying? Well, most people view the straightforward approach of saying, "Are you paying for this date or am I?" as a little inappropriate, unless, of course, you've already decided beyond a reasonable doubt that you never, ever want to see this person again. While honesty and forthrightness are considered virtues in most relationships, a first date is far too delicate a situation for such effrontery.

Thus, the best thing to do is to be prepared for all financial possibilities. In short, take money with you. This is no new trend. Our mothers called it "pin money" because they pinned enough money to their undergarments to get them home in an emergency. Pin it where you like, just bring cash.

Generally, says Dr. Polenz, who pays on the first date breaks down along gender lines. In her informal survey of nearly 200 twenty-something people who were single and dating in Manhattan (where drinks, dinner, and a movie can run $80 to $100) this was the consensus:

He says: Interestingly, the majority of Generation X men said that if they were the ones doing the asking, they felt obliged to pay for the first date and probably the next three or four ensuing dates.

Most men said that after four or five dates they felt comfortable bringing up the subject of money and who pays for what. John S. says, "I usually make a joke of it and say something like 'Look, I'm not after your money. I'm a struggling (actor, musician, stock broker) and this is what I can and cannot do financially.' What the girl can contribute moneywise will decide how often we go out. But every woman is different, and it takes four or five dates before you know someone well enough to lay your cards on the table like that."

My friend in Boston, James C., says that if he makes more money than the woman, he usually pays. But if he thinks she has the larger salary, he tends to share expenses. And how do you know what another person makes without exchanging W–2 forms? "You have a general idea. If I'm going out with a teacher, for instance, I know things are probably tight financially."

Dr. Polenz noted that a significant percentage of men expressed mixed feelings about a woman offering to split the check on the first date. They wonder: "Does she think I can't afford this? Is she just being polite, and will she really be pissed if I take her up on her offer? Is she signaling that she doesn't want to feel obligated to me in any way?"

She says: Suzy S. says that she is very sensitive to the man's financial status. "You can usually tell by his job what financial category the guy is in. If I sense things are tight for him, I might casually offer to pay for the movie tickets if he's paid for dinner; but it's tricky because some men are offended if a woman offers to pay."

Diane M., who is in her mid-twenties and has her own company, uses the following logic: "If the man is older and has a good job, I expect him to pay for everything. On the other hand, if it is a guy I really like and I know he makes less money than I do, I may try to help with some of the expenses after the first date."

Dr. Polenz's advice: A basic tenet in Relationship Development 101 is that every new couple needs a certain amount of getting-to-know-you time. For some, it can be a few days, but for most, it requires a few weeks, if not months.

If you are starting a relationship with someone and you think the relationship has real potential, do what you must to neutralize financial issues for the moment so you can "buy" more time together. Cook dinner at home. Go skating in the park. Rent a video or catch the $2 early bird show.

The time will come when you must face your financial differences. For now, check out your prospective mate's soul first to see if you are truly compatible. You'll have time to run a Dun & Bradstreet report later.

Going Steady

In the 1990s, courtship as Jane Austen knew it does not exist, and the watered-down version that remains rarely lasts more than a month. If you have made it through the I-stop-breathing-if-he/she-brushes-against-my-arm phase, congratulations! According to Dr. Polenz, you're ready to begin Stage II of coupledom, which is the move toward a more "comfortable familiarity." Now is the time to start looking for the early warning signs that you're dating a financial paraplegic.

From a money management point of view, what should you look for in a prospective mate? Probably 99.2 percent of the population falls into either the Spender or Saver category. You know in your heart, without much internal debate, which one you fall into. (It's hard-wired into your system.) If you think back over your past five dates, you've probably picked up clues as to whether your significant other is a Saver or a Spender, too. (Looking at the spending habits of his or her mother and father may tell you a lot. For instance, what did the parents give your beloved on his or her birthday? Was it a card? A trip to Sweden? Nothing? It's a clue.)

Dr. Polenz says that while opposites may attract, *partners who are most alike enjoy the highest success rate.* Does this mean Spenders should pair off only with other Spenders and Savers with Savers? "No," says Polenz, "it means that you must be aware of the repercussions of whatever financial type you choose to be with."

"The reason so much emphasis is placed on getting to know someone well over a significant period of time before one makes a lifelong commitment, is that most people can deal with problems they know about in advance, and have had time to accept. It is the surprises, and too many of them, that throw a relationship into perpetual turmoil.

"For instance, if your potential mate is color-blind, you'd better prepare yourself for a lifetime of checking for matching socks before he leaves the house. If you know that your teetotaler love has an unusual number of alcoholic relatives, you need to decide if you are the type of person who could deal with this problem, should it develop later on," says Dr. Polenz.

Dr. Polenz's advice: *Notice the little things.* It's the small details that will tip you off as to what kind of person your partner is. Does he or she meticulously count the change after every transaction, even if it means holding up the line? Is he or she an extravagant tipper, even when the service sucked? When you go Dutch, does he or she split the check fifty-fifty or take out a calculator to add up your expenses to the penny?

Things like this, if observed repeatedly over a period of time, can reveal much about your partner's financial behavior. Don't get hung up on occasional quirkiness. We're all entitled to a few eccentricities. Focus on the pattern you see developing. If something happens moneywise with your prospective significant other that disturbs you, Dr. Polenz suggests asking yourself this question: Was the behavior appropriate to the situation? For instance, say you accidentally bumped into your love interest jogging in the park and decided to go for drinks. He or she may have been without a wallet and had to lean on you for cash. Perfectly understandable. On the other hand, suppose you make a date to meet for pizza and your love interest brings his or her entire Little League soccer team, then disappears when the check arrives.

"The question is, did this leave a bad taste in your mouth?" says Dr. Polenz. "If the behavior was unfriendly or ungenerous at a time when he or she could afford to be magnanimous, then you have grounds for concern."

Is this helpful? Then keep reading and remember that the knife cuts both ways. While you are busy making mental notes on his or her financial moves, your partner may be doing the same with you.

The Perfect Financial Couple

Can a spender and a saver find true (financial) happiness? Augusta and Ray Martin have. "We keep each other in check. Ray has inspired me to take control of my spending sprees and I think I've loosened up the hard-core saver in him. The other day he actually bought a shirt he really liked but didn't absolutely need!" says Augusta.

Like many couples, the Martins lived together for almost five years before marrying three tears ago. They are expecting their first child in a few months. During their living-together years, the couple kept their finances separate. "Pooling finances requires a very high trust level, and I didn't want to rush into that," says Augusta.

"Ray also wanted to loan me the money to pay off my student loan debt, which was an enormous burden to me because I wasn't making much money. But I just couldn't do it. I felt if the relationship didn't work out, I didn't want to be left owing this guy thousands of dollars." After they were married and began pooling their money, Augusta accepted Ray's offers to pay off the loans which saved several hundred dollars in interest payments. She then repaid the loan to him out of her personal expenses budget.

Even though Ray is the financial expert, Augusta has always been the bill-payer to insure her involvement in their finances. "I learned a lot. The first time Ray and I bought a house together, he made me arrange all the financing so I would understand the process. It was a great experience."

And how many credit cards do the Martins have? One. A Visa which gives each of them a card with their name on it, but under one account. "We put all expenses, groceries, dry-cleaning, gasoline, everything we can on the credit card. I don't even have my department store cards anymore. Then we carry just enough cash to buy lunch and cover parking meters. It works out great! At the end of the month, we're able to track our expenses to the penny," Augusta says.

Living Together 101

So, you've gotten past the first date, moved beyond going steady, and have decided to try cohabitation. For better or worse, you are entering into a relationship for which there is no traditional financial structure or format to follow. *Unmarried couples do not have the same financial advantages and legal protection as married couples.* The good news is that two can live as cheaply as one. The bad news is you're back to the ever-unpopular question, "Who pays?"

The goal is to prepare yourself legally and financially in case your cohabitation does not work out. Be real with yourself. Remember, if you've been with your sweetheart for some period of time, breaking up is likely to be every bit as emotionally devastating as a divorce. Financially, it can be even more disastrous and take longer to recover from.

On that happy note, let's move on to the first really hard decision the two of you have to make: Where will you live? If you can negotiate through this issue successfully so that neither partner feels cheated, there is real hope for the future.

Dr. Polenz's advice: Let's assume you and your significant other have already determined that your relationship bears no resemblance to that of Felix and Oscar, and you're prepared to make the compromises necessary to cohabit. The ideal scenario, says Dr. Polenz, is for each of you to give up your respective homes and find a new place together. It's difficult for Person A to move into Person B's space, particularly if Person B has lived there alone for some time. Plus, a new place gives the relationship a fresh start. Ideally, it should be one that, in the event of a breakup, either one of you could afford on your own.

In the case where one partner owns a house and the other rents, the decision is usually predetermined; it's easier to give up a rental than to sell a house. If you are both home owners, then one or both of you will have to sell or rent your house. If both of you currently rent, there may be a compelling reason why one of you should move into the other's apartment (the rent is less, there's more room, the lease is unbreakable, etc.).

Whatever the decision, you both need to understand and plan for the consequences of a breakup. *Discuss this early while the bloom is still on the rose.* You don't want to come home from work to find that a morning quarrel with your partner has resulted in the changing of locks and the boxing up of your belongings.

So you've found a mutually acceptable address? Congratulations! Here are additional guidelines from Dr. Polenz:

1. Learn how to negotiate.

Let's says it's Friday night, and you've had a particularly difficult week at work. You're really looking forward to relaxing over a candlelight dinner in a nice restaurant. Your better half, who insists you cannot afford this extravagance, prefers to hit the drive thru for a bag of burgers, then settle in for a night of television. Before you know it, you're in a screaming match over who wastes the most money and who is the biggest bore in the world. What to do?

Dr. Polenz's advice: Welcome to one of the most time-honored lovers' rituals of this century—fights over money. Most arguments about finances are, in actuality, about something else. But when you're in the thick of it, you think you'll never be able to work things out (and maybe you won't). However, there are steps you can take to cut down on the frequency of money-related fights and the potential damage they can cause.

Before you can effectively negotiate a truce, you need to understand why you're driving each other crazy. Recognize where your financial hot buttons are and why your partner's behavior pushes them. There are three general factors that affect our attitudes about money. The first is your financial personality type (Spender or Saver). There may be some room for change, but it's unrealistic to hope for a complete turnaround. In theory, you addressed this issue during your dating phase. You know which financial personality type you are and which one your partner is. You've moved forward with the relationship because you believe you can handle your differences, right? A Spender and a Saver can cohabit, but they must learn to understand and appreciate each other's financial strengths and weaknesses.

The second factor influencing your attitude about money is your family's financial behavior. Undoubtedly your parents' habits with money had a hand in shaping yours. Now go back and think about how they've colored your view of your mate's financial practices.

The third attitude-adjusting factor is your preconceived notion of how a partner should behave. Are you expecting your mate to be Prince or Princess Charming twenty-four hours a day? Are you angry that he or she doesn't know how to kiss it and make it all better? Be honest with yourself: Are your expectations realistic?

Understanding your own financial quirks will help you deal more objectively and compassionately with those of your mate. If you each know where the other is coming from, it will be easier to meet in the middle. It also should help you establish more realistic expectations of one another so you don't set yourselves up for a fall.

2. Agree on how to split household expenses.

This may seem like nit-picking, but remember, the more you and your future partner can work out before moving in together, the fewer surprises—and fights—you'll have later. Follow these steps for splitting your expenses effectively:

Make a list of household expenses. He may feel that tampons do not go under the heading of household expenses; likewise, she may not want the $29.95 Pay-Per-View charge for the World Wrestling Extravaganza in this category.

Determine who is financially responsible for what. If both partners earn about the same salary, splitting the bills evenly may be the easiest solution. However, if there is significant inequity in your incomes, you will need to negotiate a different split.

Decide how the bills will be paid. Do you each assume certain payments or do you designate one partner the accountant to whom the other must write a check for his or her portion of the monthly expenses? Either way, pledge to each other that no bill will go unpaid for more than one month. If one of you can't pay a bill on time, discuss it with your partner before the electricity is shut off.

One suggestion here: See if you can delicately find out if your significant other is creditworthy (i.e., his or her credit report is okay). If his or her credit rating sucks, it might be better for you to be the bill payer.

Set up a system of financial accountability that ensures the timely payment of all bills. I know she can turn the world on with her smile; I'm aware that his financial dealings are as impeccable as his manners. Don't be stupid. Every four seconds somebody's ex-lover takes off owing eight months of back rent.

3. Keep score, but don't nickel-and-dime each other.

Understand the difference between keeping score and "keeping score." "I once knew a very easygoing, likable chap who said the reason he was divorcing his wife of seven years was 'because she ate up all the ice cream,'" says Dr. Polenz. "Obviously that wasn't the entire reason, but quite often I have seen otherwise inconsequential events, like routinely polishing off the last of the ice cream and not replacing it, become the straw that breaks a partner's back."

The bottom line is that living together, even marriage, does not release either partner from the rules of common courtesy. If you borrow $50 from your partner until payday, return the money to him or her when you cash your check. Don't think for a moment that he or she will forget.

4. Move into pooling finances slowly.

Putting both partner's money into one pot, such as a joint checking account, is a major step in your financial relationship. You must both exhibit a high level of trust and confidence to make this a success, particularly without the legal protection of marriage. The moment you pool your money with another person, it gives your partner the power to question your every expenditure (and vice versa). Is your relationship ready for this?

Keep in mind that a growing number of couples never move to the one-pot style of money management. Even after they are married, they maintain separate checking accounts, retirement funds, etc., because they say it significantly cuts down on arguments over money. My friend's aunt and uncle have been married for more than fifty-four years and still split every household bill and restaurant tab. It's what works for them.

The advantage of a joint checking account is that one partner can write a check in the other partner's absence. The danger of a joint checking account is that one partner can write a check in the other partner's absence. Unless you have a compelling reason to join funds (a child who must be provided for or a partner who frequently travels) move slowly. Start with pooling some of your disposable income into a cookie jar or piggy bank at home. Pledge to use it only for emergencies or mutually agreed-upon splurges, like paying for Girl Scout cookies or sending out for pizza. See how that goes for a few months.

Finally, consider that a joint checking account may be overkill. If you need funds from an absent partner, you can always get a post-dated check.

5. Neither a borrower nor a lender be.

This doesn't apply to your mate's request for a bus token or a $20 loan until payday. If you're the borrower, don't trivialize the importance of prompt repayment just because the loan is small.

Borrowing or lending a large sum of money to a mate has a couple damaging effects. First, it puts a significant strain on the relationship for one partner to be strongly beholden to the other. And if that isn't tension-evoking enough, guess what happens if the relationship suddenly ends? Figuratively, it's like paying taxes on a house that has already burned to the ground.

6. Do not forsake your financial religion.

Don't think you can blow off the first half of this book just because you've found Mr. or Ms. Perfect. Do not forget your master plan. Adjust, but do not abandon, your short- and long-term financial goals, and above all, do not leave your budget on the closet shelf of your old apartment.

Living Together 201

At some point, probably after the first year or so of living together, you need to evaluate your relationship and decide if your partner is someone with whom you are going to build a long-term future. This is a future that might include big financial commitments, like children, cars, a home, 401(k) plans, and retirement funds. At this point, the legal and financial ramifications of living together become more dangerous.

Am I sounding melodramatic? Consider this abbreviated list of what unmarried partners are not entitled to under the law:

- In an emergency, you cannot make medical decisions for your partner.

- If your partner dies, his or her next-of-kin, not you, will inherit all of your partner's money, property, and possessions.

- You cannot share each other's health insurance or company pension plans.

- In most states, unmarried (or homosexual) partners of people with children are denied parental rights, including the right to make medical decisions for a child in an emergency.

So, life gets complicated. If you are in your sophomore or junior year of living together, then it is time to make the legal arrangements that will provide both of you with lasting security.

Renting With The Option to Buy

According to a recent University of Wisconsin study, three out of five couples, or about 60%, will marry after living together for a year or more. However, according to the same study, the divorce rate is higher among couples who have lived together before marriage than for twosomes who have not (36% versus 27%).

Quiz—Are You Dating a Financial Paraplegic?

With your current love interest in mind, ask yourself the following questions:

1. Does he or she insist on expensive, chic restaurants most of the time? [Potential User if you're paying or even going halfsies]

2. Is he or she slow to pay back a modest loan? [Flaky at best, User at worst]

3. Is he or she annoyed if you offer to split the check? [Control Freak who thinks you're a financial idiot]

4. Is he or she appalled that you could spend $165 on CDs? [Miser or Control Freak]

5. Has he or she "forgotten" her wallet more than three times and looked to you to pick up the tab? [Flaky at best, User at worse]

6. Has he or she repeatedly implied that your car sucks and that the real you belongs in a $33,000 BMW? [User—and that's a 6.5 on the Materialistic Richter Scale]

7. Does he or she go to the rest room moments before the waiter or bartender brings the check? [Pick one: Flaky/Miser/User]

8. Does the subject of how much more money your counterparts are making surface frequently? [Potential User]

9. Is he or she consistently unavailable when significant dates (your birthday, Valentine's Day, New Year's, etc.) roll around? [Miser]

10. Is clipping coupons, particularly the early bird or 2-for-1 restaurant coupons, a vital part of his or her weekly routine? [Sprouting Miser]

Scoring: According to Dr. Polenz, if you answered "yes" to five or more questions, run like hell. No matter how cute he or she is, you've drawn a lemon. If you answered "yes" to four or fewer questions, beware. There are storm warnings out on this person. And if you answered "no" to all questions, give the potential mate an A for consideration and generosity. There's real hope here.

CHAPTER 12

Money and Marriage: Who Pays?

If you are engaged, you should consider a prenuptial agreement. Sound wild? Even the suggestion of such a thing certainly was a few years ago. Prenups were for the Donald Trump crowd only. Not today. While they are not in universal use yet, prenups are growing in popularity with people of all economic levels and most likely will be commonplace in the next century.

Why are prenuptial agreements appealing? Anyone over the age of nine knows someone who has suffered from a divorce. A prewedding legal agreement outlines premarital property and specifies how assets are to be divided if the marriage ends. This can minimize the confusion and bitterness of a breakup. In some instances, a prenup may even help prevent a divorce by forcing a couple to address difficult financial and emotional issues before they get married.

Here are some of the issues a prenuptial agreement can address:

Common Issues Dealt With In A Prenuptial Agreement

by Meridith J. Bronson, Esq.

- *Identification and treatment of premarital property*
- *Adjusting rights that may have accrued prior to marriage during periods of cohabitation*
- *Providing for the right to use, manage, control, or dispose of property during marriage*
- *Establishing a manner for division or distribution of property upon separation, divorce, or death*
- *Setting forth financial benefits in lieu of property distribution*
- *Estate planning and disposition of estate upon death*
- *Spousal support upon separation/divorce or elimination/waiver of support*
- *Designation of alternate guardian in event of incapacity (prenuptial agreement cannot be used to affect child support or custody)*

Each party should consult a separate and independent attorney well in advance of the planned wedding date. This provides time for necessary disclosure, analysis and negotiation. It also dilutes the possibility of claims of duress and allows for the resolution of important issues without the added stress of an imminent wedding date.

Newsweek, 1995 [Special advertising section]

Think carefully before you dismiss prenuptial agreements as being too sophisticated for your needs. The two of you may be young and financially flatlined right now, but consider what you bring to the marriage, besides a modest bank account and your mother's old china. You may not want to divide it as community property if the marriage fails in two years. Think, for instance, about your antique doll or baseball card collection. It's worth a great deal of money, but you'd never consider selling, unless forced to do so through divorce settlement. Do you stand to inherit your great uncle's sheep farm one day? Do your parents carry a life insurance policy that could be cashed out for an impressive sum? These are things you may want to protect.

The first step in creating a prenup is for each partner to make a list of his or her assets and liabilities. All the experts encourage full disclosure in this process—without it the prenuptial agreement will be incomplete, inaccurate and basically useless. Next, the couple should sit down and decide what will be addressed in the agreement, including how assets and liabilities are to be handled during the marriage and in the event of a breakup. Some couples are extremely creative with their prenuptial agreements, including points well outside the financial arena, like how often they will have sex each week, who will take out the trash (him, of course!), and the maximum number of hours a spouse may watch football. One couple even mandated that the grocery shopping would always be done with a shopping list!

Have initial discussions about your agreement privately. The more you can hammer out on your own, the less your legal expenses will be. However, when it comes time to draw up the agreement, it is imperative that each of you have your own independent attorney who will look out for your best interests. Godspeed.

How To Set Up Financial Housekeeping

When two people get married they form a corporation of sorts. The two partners combine their resources, and each contributes, in his or her own way, to the growth of their new "company." With hard work and a dash of luck, they have an excellent chance to build an impressive empire, one that will provide for themselves and their children.

The first thing any new company needs is a solid business plan. Just as you did this for yourself in Chapters 2 and 3, now you need to repeat the process with your teammate. This means long-term goals and a day-to-day budget designed to help you reach them. The difference now, however, is that you both may have some hard questions to answer. For instance, who pays when one partner comes into the marriage with large debts like school loans, credit card bills or alimony? Who pays if one partner works and the other doesn't, or if one makes significantly more money than the other? Who pays for the care of children from another relationship? These are decisions the two of you will have to work out.

The first two money management choices that need to be made are:

1. How do you want to manage your money?

2. Who takes on the role of accountant?

There are three commonly used styles of money management to consider as you set up financial housekeeping. They are: (1) the traditional system of pooling both partners' money into one account; (2) the modern method, in which each partner maintains his or her own accounts and responsibility for the bills is divvied up; and (3) a combination of the traditional and the modern methods. Which one you choose often depends on what stage of life you and your partner are in, your plans for the future, and whether or not you have children.

Choosing the accountant, the partner who takes on paying the bills and keeping track of expenses, is usually the easier decision. Chances are one of you has more experience or a stronger willingness to take on the chore than the other. (When you go to divvy up household chores, however, the accountant's job counts as three.)

Even though one partner becomes the official accountant, both partners must be aware at all times of the family's financial status and how the money management system works. You may not be responsible for the day-to-day bill paying, but you still must know all of the nitty-gritty specifics, as well as have an understanding of the big financial picture. If you doubt the importance of this, check with one of the many widows whose home went into foreclosure because she didn't even know where the key to the desk was when her spouse suddenly died.

Here are examples of how two modern couples handle their finances:

Chris and Gena, both under twenty-five, saved scrupulously for one year to put a down payment on a small starter home in Queens where they could have more room for their nineteen-month-old son. Both work, he at an auto body shop, she as an office manager; both earn similar salaries totaling about $47,000 a year.

The couple decided to try living on Chris's slightly larger salary and putting Gena's pay into a savings account. "We pretend my salary doesn't exist," says Gena. Their plan is to buy a larger home in a nicer neighborhood within the next two or three years, then rent out the first for extra revenue.

Each partner has an individual bank account, and they share a joint account that is dedicated solely to paying the mortgage. Either partner can make a deposit, but not withdrawals. Gena makes the mortgage payments, but Chris can make them if needed.

The couple, both devout Quicken fans, lived on a tight budget and built up $2,300 in an emergency fund. Then, Gena's grandfather in South America fell gravely ill. Fortunately, the couple's good financial habits allowed them to make this important unexpected trip. "It wiped out our savings, but it didn't put us in debt. We'll build it back again before too long," says Gena.

Jim and Jane, on the other hand, have been married for three years and are a little older, thirty-one and twenty-eight respectively. Both have very good jobs, although Jim, as a pediatrician, earns about forty percent more than Jane. They hope to start a family in the next year or so.

When they were first married, Jim, the family accountant, says the couple pooled their salaries into one account. "It was a disaster. We never knew what the other had spent or even what the correct balance was. Both of us had lived on our own for too long to start informing someone every time we wrote a check."

Learning from their mistake, Jim and Jane found that to avoid arguments, it was better to keep separate checking accounts and to divvy up the bills. Now, Jim covers the mortgage and all insurance payments, pays for his clothes and his car payment, and picks up the check when they go out for the evening. Jane pays the bills for the utilities, cable TV, her clothes, her car payment, and most of the groceries. (Jim likes to shop at the farmer's market on Saturdays and pays for this himself.) Each contributes the maximum possible to a pension plan and pays for his or her own company-sponsored health care plan. If one partner has cash flow problems, the other covers. "I pay it back, she doesn't," laughs Jim.

Jim and Jane do share one thing—a joint savings account. Each has pledged to contribute 7.5 percent of his or her annual salary. Jim pays it in one lump sum; Jane contributes quarterly. They have agreed to meet with a financial planner to work out a more sophisticated long-range plan.

The one area that requires constant vigilance by both parties is the considerable temptation Jane's job offers. As an executive in the advertising department of a major department store, Jane gets between twenty and fifty percent off any item in the store. Jim explains, "[The temptation] is hardest on Jane. She hears about the upcoming sales from the ads, and she has to walk through the store to get in or out of her office. I'm not much help because I walk in the store, see something on sale and think, 'Cool, I can get this through Jane for forty percent off retail.' Employees are by far this store's best customers."

Through exceptional self-discipline, Jane has implemented a couple of behavior modification measures. She makes herself leave through a back elevator of the store and tries not to peruse the merchandise at lunch time. She has set a $500 limit on her department store credit card, and she leaves it at home most of the time.

"We still argue occasionally about money, and I'm probably guilty of rolling my eyes when I see her come home with yet another new set of china, but no one draws blood. As long as the bills are paid and money is going into long-term savings, we respect the other's right to waste a little bit of money," says Jim.

What both of these couples have learned (and you and your spouse can, too) is how to customize their financial lives so they (1) don't kill each other and (2) can build a real future together.

Legal Agreements That Provide Lasting Security

Document	Purpose	Cost*
Will	Makes sure your partner receives property when you die. Without a will, all assets are transferred automatically to your next of kin. Essential for couples with children to help partner get custody if legal parent dies.	$100–$300
Trust	Protects wishes of deceased if family members are likely to contest the will. Also has significant tax benefits for couples with complicated estates.	$500–$1,500
Relationship Agreement	Ensures that both parties agree on handling of joint property, shared debt, and household finances. Also, outlines what will happen if couple splits up.	$600–$1,000
Real Estate Agreement	Establishes how title will be held and mortgage and maintenance paid. Also decides what will happen to property if relationship dissolves. Can be included with a general relationship agreement.	$600–$1,500
Parenting Agreement	Outlines for each partner the support obligations and decision-making rights with regard to a child. Also may define how families of each partner will relate to the child. In the event of a breakup, outlines visitation rights and support obligations. Such agreements may not hold up in court.	$600–$1,500
Durable Power of Attorney	Gives domestic partner the right to make any financial decisions should one partner become mentally or physically incapacitated. Otherwise the next of kin has that right.	$100–$300
Health Care Proxy	Allows one partner to make medical decisions should the other become sick or injured. Also allows partner to consult with doctors and visit in hospital. A living will may also be advised.	$100–$300

How To Handle A Spouse's Debts

Another financial challenge the two of you will need to face is any substantial debt that one or both of you bring to the marriage.

In a perfect world, both partners would come into the relationship with little to no debt. Okay, this is the real world. The next best scenario is that both come with about the same (small) amount of debt. Things get sticky when one partner brings a considerable amount of debt to the marriage. Whether it is good debt from a school loan that paid for a master's degree or bad debt from too many clothes charged on credit cards, it doesn't really matter. You still have to resolve the problem.

Sit down with your beloved and decide how, within your budget, the two of you are going to eliminate this debt. Do your very best to evoke Golden Rule No. 2, Emotion is the Enemy, before you have this conversation. If it is an ongoing debt, like overuse of credit cards, cauterize the bleeding vein. Then treat the debt as a line item expense and decide whether one or both of you will contribute to pay it off. Remember, if the debt consists of credit card charges, it may be best for both of you to whittle it down. The faster you pay it off, the less money you lose to interest charges.

How To Prepare Financially For The Stork

It is best not to focus too long on the exact cost of raising a child from birth until the age of eighteen. The species may die out if this information falls into the wrong hands. Really want to know? Okay, brace yourself. According to the newest figures from the U.S. Department of Agriculture, the average parent will spend $132,660 (excluding college, which might be another $100,000) on each child.

Somehow, most people manage the costs of parenthood, and so will you. If you've already proven that you can set up and implement a real-life budget with flexibility and you can handle emergencies because you've built up an impressive nest egg, then the only worry left is picking out the baby's name.

Just to be sure your financial house is in order, here is a brief rerun of those Manage-to-Grow-Money System techniques we've already discussed:

- Start shoveling hard into savings. The effort is never wasted. Even if there are no crippling emergencies and the child earns a full, four-year scholarship to Smith, you can use the money to buy a vacation home in the Bahamas.

- Eliminate debt. Whatever you were spending on debt you now will need for diapers and child care. Whittle this down so your newborn won't notice what a goofus you've been with credit cards.

- Check your health care and insurance plans. Your health care plan obviously needs to cover a new child, and your life insurance needs to cover your income, or the extra cost of child care, should something happen to you or your spouse.

- Start a college savings account in your child's name. There are certain tax breaks on savings held in a child's name. Get the full scoop from your accountant.

- Revise your will to provide for your child and name a guardian. These are ugly things to have to think about in the midst of such happiness, but for the sake of your child, you must. You need an official legal document, traditionally a will, that specifies your wishes, including who you would choose to care for your child, should something happen to you and your spouse. Make sure that your attorney and a close relative or friend have a copy of your revised will. Remember, this is an unpleasant decision, but it is yours to make.

HOW MUCH DOES IT COST TO RAISE A CHILD?

A BUNDLE! The table below illustrates how much Mom and Dad spend on a child from birth to a age 18. Calculations assume two children in a family and are for the younger child, but you can apply them to the older child, too. For an only child, multiply the totals by 1.26. And for a family with three children or more, multiply the totals by 0.78 to find out how much is spent on each child.

		Total Spent Over 18 Years For:							
Annual Income	Annual Spending for First Three Years	All Expenses	Housing	Food	Transportation	Clothing	Health Care	Child Care & Education	Other*
Less than $32,000	$4,960	$97,710	$30,540	$19,650	$16,530	$9,330	$6,840	$5,790	$9,030
$32,000-$54,100	6,870	132,660	43,020	23,700	23,070	10,860	8,460	9,840	13,710
More than $54,100	10,210	192,780	69,780	30,270	27,750	14,370	10,050	16,590	23,970

* Other expenses include personal-care items, entertainment and reading material. Source: U.S. Department of Agriculture, Agricultural Research Service

Kiplinger's Personal Finance Magazine March 1995

What You Need To Know Financially About Divorce

Anyone who has ever been through a divorce and lived to talk about it understands that this is a unique trauma. "After the smoke has cleared, most people would be hard pressed to choose which is worse, the emotional devastation or the financial ruin. Both can take years to recover from," says Dr. Polenz.

While marriage is rooted in love, divorce is centered on money. Splitting up means dividing your house and all its possessions, your cash, your debts, and even your children's time. Here is a brief summary of what happens:

Common Issues Dealt With In Divorce
by Meridith J. Bronson, Esq.

A property settlement and support agreement sets [sic] forth agreed-upon rights and obligations of spouses upon divorce. It addresses the three significant financial issues that must be resolved upon dissolution of a marriage: alimony, child support, and division of property.

As a rule, alimony is tax deductible for the paying spouse and considered taxable income for the receiving spouse. Child support is not. By considering tax rates, exemptions for children, and other factors, the divorcing couple can maximize their assets. Advice from an attorney and/or accountant can help.

A three-tier analysis is appropriate when dealing with asset distribution:

Tier 1: *What assets are to be divided. Good premarital planning and record keeping help identify assets. Documentation of assets, source of funds, and acquisition dates are key elements.*

Tier 2: *What assets are worth. This often includes valuation experts and/or accountants to assist in valuing businesses, goodwill, and other intangible assets. Bank and brokerage statements, employee benefit statements, and other readily available records are helpful sources.*

Tier 3: *The amount and manner of asset division and distribution. Even if state law or agreement between spouses provides for equal division of assets, the manner of distribution is critical.*

Failure to approach distribution prudently can prove costly. A spouse who wishes to retain the marital home should consider hidden costs such as capital gains. Retirement benefits can be divided in a way to avoid tax consequences. Ideally, the divorcing parties will end up with a diversified financial portfolio, minimum anxiety, and a fresh start on the future.

Newsweek, 1995 [Special advertising section]

An Affordable Divorce Settlement?

The one financial issue that seems to stick in the craw of all divorcees is cost. As one veteran of the war says, "The $30,000 we paid the divorce lawyers could have gone toward putting our kids through college, not theirs."

In her article, "Don't Let Divorce Kill or Bankrupt You," (*The New York Post*, November 19, 1996), Marsha McCreadie describes an alternative to divorce lawyers that is gaining popularity, both for its reduced cost and reduced bloodshed.

The alternative is called private arbitration. The divorcing couple choose a qualified arbitrator from a list, and the arbitrator, often an ex-judge, works out the division of property and assets. The arbitrator's decision is final. However, the arbitrator can make child support decisions, but not child custody rulings.

The arbitrator route may be ideal for no-fault divorces where the couple has reached a mutual decision and retains some hope of remaining friends. The fees are far less. The average middle class divorce through two attorneys can run $5,000 to $30,000 per person while an arbitrator averages $1,500 to $4,000 per couple.

For a list of arbitrators in your area, call the American Arbitration Association at (212) 484-4000.

Premarital Counseling Options

Moved by the fact that half the couples they married later divorced, a growing number of priests, rabbis, and clergymen are using a new system designed to strengthen couples' communication skills and ability to handle conflict. PREPARE (Premarital Personal and Relationship Evaluation) is a 125-question evaluation that addresses issues ranging from whether your intended spouse will make a good parent to how enjoyable you find your prospective mate's favorite leisure activities. For a list of PREPARE counselors and clergy, call (800) 331-1661.

Additionally, both the American Psychological Association, (202) 336-5500, and the American Association of Marriage and Family Therapists, (202) 452-0109, offer names of affordable professional counselors and psychotherapists in your area who specialize in premarital counseling.

CHAPTER 13

Encyclopedia of Financial Terms

abatement   An exemption from paying penalties on late taxes.

account   A record of the changes in an accounting item, such as cash, inventory, or sales.

accountant   A person trained in one or more fields of accounting. A certified public accountant (CPA) practices accounting through auditing and expressing an opinion if a company's statements followed generally accepted accounting principles (GAAP).

accounts receivable   The money that is owed to a company from the sale of their goods or services.

accumulated depreciation   The total depreciation recorded for an asset since its date of acquisition.

acid test   Called the acid-test ratio or the quick ratio, it measures how many time current assets (minus inventories) can pay current liabilities. It is a measure of a company's ability to meet current obligations.

actuary   The person who calculates all those charts of risks and costs for insurance, called actuarial tables. Actuarial tables produced by actuaries show life expectancies for different age groups and desirable weights for different ages and heights.

adjustable rate mortgage (ARM)   A mortgage with an interest rate that may change, or adjust, periodically (say, every one to three years) during the life of the loan and is tied to some index or formula. It usually has a low first-year rate, which is also known as an introductory rate.

adjusted gross income (AGI)   Gross income minus any above-the-line deductions.

adjuster   The insurance company employee who settles the amount the company will pay for a claim.

ADV form (investment advisor)   The SEC (Securities and Exchange Commission) form that generally describes the investment portion of what a particular financial planner does and how that planner is compensated. If a financial planner wishes to give investment advice he or she must be registered with the SEC by completing the ADV form. Once registered, the planner is then a Registered Investment Advisor (RIA). Part II of the ADV form can be requested by an individual who wishes to use the services of the financial planner.

after-tax income   Income after taxes have been deducted or paid.

agent   In the simplest terms, a person who has been given authority to act on someone else's behalf.

aggressive growth fund   A mutual fund seeking maximum capital gains and not current income. See mutual funds.

agreement of sale   A written contract between a buyer and a seller that comes before the actual closing takes place. It lays out all the terms that they have agreed upon for the sale to close.

air rights   The rights of owners to the air above lands. These rights may come into conflict with the rights of the public for "paths in the sky" for airplanes.

alimony   Payments made from one former spouse to another due to separation or divorce.

allocation of resources   This is one of the key factors in economics: how a limited amount of resources (both physical resources and employees) are dispersed among the people and companies who need them to make products and services, and then how products and services get from the producer to the consumers.

allowances   By specifying the number of withholding allowances on the W-4 form, your company computes how much taxes to withhold from your paycheck. The fewer allowances, the larger your paycheck, but don't forget this is only an estimate. If not enough taxes are withheld you may owe a penalty, besides the additional taxes.

American Stock Exchange (Amex)   The American Stock Exchange. The American Stock Exchange is the second-oldest stock exchange in the United States. Founded in 1842 (originally called the New York Curb Exchange because business was actually done on the street curb), its rival is the New York Stock Exchange (NYSE). Wall Street, New York City, is the home to both the AMEX and the NYSE.

amortization; amortize   To write off gradually and systematically over time. For instance, an accountant amortizes the cost of an asset through depreciation.

annual benefit statement   A report generated for each employee at the end of the year showing the specific benefits of the company for that employee. It also serves to advertise what the company has contributed to these various benefits. Usually the benefit statement will summarize such items as the total amount employees have invested in the 401(k) and pension plans and the amounts the company contributed to them, and the medical and life insurance programs and how much it costs the company to provide those benefits.

annual percentage rate (APR)   The amount—as a percentage—of the interest paid each year. Even if an advertisement screams out "2 percent monthly interest!" it must report the APR (here, 26.82 percent) as well.

annual report   Companies provide annual reports for their investors. They are pretty much what you'd expect—a report on the company's status: what the company did the year before, their ideas and business outlook, a full financial report including a balance sheet and a summary of the audit done by a public accounting firm. Because they are designed to make investors feel all warm and cozy about their investments, annual reports are usually big, glossy productions.

annuity   1. A standard form of a pension payout, a stream of equal monthly payments for the rest of the retiree's life. This is in contrast to a lump-sum payout. For the different forms of payouts from pensions, see pension payouts. 2. Term insurance that can be renewed by you year-by-year.

appraisal   An unbiased estimate of a property's value. Most banks require a real estate appraisal before they will give a mortgage on the property. The lender usually refers to the result of this appraisal as "the appraised value."

appreciation   Any increase in a property's value.

appropriation   An amount set aside for a specific business purpose.

arbitrage   Buying an investment or commodity in one market and selling in another market in order to make a profit.

arrears   If something is overdue, it is said to be in arrears.

asset   Any property with value; may refer to real estate, investments, or personal property.

asset allocation   Determining the percentage of each broad category of investments in a portfolio. For instance, 50 percent large cap stocks, 40 percent intermediate bonds, and 10 percent money market funds each would be an example of an asset allocation. It is considered the basic strategy of a portfolio. As that category performs, so goes your portfolio. Definable categories in stocks include: large cap, mid-cap, small cap, and international stocks. Categories in bonds include long corporate and treasury bonds, intermediate corporate and treasury bonds, high yield (junk bonds), and municipal bonds. Categories in money market include taxable and non-taxable funds.

at the money   When an option's strike price for a call or a put is exactly the price of the underlying security, the option is said to be at the money. That is, it is not out of the money (you haven't made money yet) or in the money (you've made money), it is just at the point of making money or not.

ATM (Automated Teller Machine)   You need an ATM card linked to one or more bank accounts to use an ATM. These machines allow you to do many of the things you used to stand on line at a bank to do—withdraw money, deposit money, transfer funds from one account to another, etcetera. Many banks are now part of huge systems (for example MAC, NYCE, or CIRRUS) that allow you to use ATMs at banks other than your own.

audit   1. The most dreaded word in the language of taxes: The Internal Revenue Service audits, or examines, a number of tax returns each year. This whole process is designed to check all the numbers you have reported to ensure the income tax payment is correct. Several things might trigger an audit: unusually high deductions, unusually low income, unusual entries, etc. Some taxpayers are chosen for auditing completely at random. 2. An accountant's review of the books and financial statements of a company. The accuracy of transactions is tested and samples are verified to determine if generally accepted accounting principles (GAAP) were followed.

auditor An accountant who performs an audit of a portion or the entirety of a company's books. The auditor's work allows investors to have confidence that the company's statements can be relied upon for analysis.

auto insurance A general form of insurance covering auto accidents, specially medical expenses and body repairs to the car.

baby bells The seven regional telephone companies created when AT&T was broken up in 1984. The original consent decree creating the Baby Bells gave them a monopoly over local phone service but banned them from participating in the long-distance or equipment manufacturing business. AT&T was excluded front the local phone business in return. Over time these distinctions have been eroded. The seven Baby Bells are: NYNEX in the Northeast, Bell Atlantic in the Mid-Atlantic states, BELLSOUTH in the South; SBC (Southwestern Bell Corporation) in the Southwest; Ameritech in the Midwest; U.S. West in the Rocky Mountains states, and Pacific Telesis in the West.

bad debt An accounts receivable that is uncollectible because of a customer's inability or unwillingness to pay.

back-end load A load is a commission charged on a mutual fund. Sometimes there is no initial sales charge—it is assessed when you sell. This is referred to as a back-end load, redemption fee, deferred sales charge, or exit fee.

balanced fund A mutual fund of stocks and bonds, in other words, balanced. Commonly stocks comprise about 60 percent of the fund while the remaining 40 percent are bonds, with some cash, or money market funds.

balance of payments The accounting of the flow of goods and money from one country to another. In the aggregate, it is the accounting of all the money that flows into and out of an economy. If we in the United States buy more goods from Japan, then Japanese businesses received more dollars during the year than

American businesses received in yen. We have more Japanese goods, they have more American dollars. The balance of payments is divided into two: the current account, which refers to the goods, and the capital account, which refers to the money.

balance of trade   The difference between exports and imports for a given country at a given time. If the country exports more than it imports, it has a favorable balance of trade. If it imports more, the balance is unfavorable.

balance sheet   A key financial statement listing all a company's assets balanced against its liabilities and stockholder equity. It represents the financial condition of a company at a particular point in time, usually at the end of the year, whereas an income statement shows the results of a company's operation over a period of time, such as a year. The balance sheet shows the assets of the company on the left, which are its productive assets, balanced by its liabilities and equity on the right, which are the claims against the company.

bank failure   The bankruptcy of a bank. Although an uncommon event, thank goodness, during the 1980s the Thrifts Savings and Loan banks failed at an alarming rate. The organization overseeing them, the FSLIC (Federal Savings and Loan Insurance Corporation) itself became insolvent in 1989 and was taken over by the main banking regulatory organization, the FDIC (Federal Deposit Insurance Corporation). The RTC (Resolution Trust Corporation) was set up to temporarily deal with this crisis, which it did.

banking   The business of accepting money as deposits and then lending money to other businesses and individuals.

bankruptcy   When an individual or company does not have enough money to pay its debts. Chapter 11 bankruptcy is voluntary bankruptcy; chapter 7 is involuntary. In either case, a court helps the company or individual to settle debts.

barriers to entry   Factors which tend to prevent or make difficult the entry of other companies into a market, usually because of existing advantages to particular companies. These factors may be economies of scale, patents, or rights to certain raw materials.

Barron's   A popular weekly publication for professional and active investors on all aspects of investments and the economy.

barter The exchange of goods without the exchange of money, only goods in kind.

base-year analysis   A method of analyzing economic trends that uses one year as the yardstick against which all others are measured. Using the "constant dollars" from one year allows analysts to see how much things have gone up or down, without inflation.

bear; bear market   A market characterized by falling prices or an investor who acts with the expectation that prices will fall.

bedroom community   A community outside a major city, from which many residents commute to the city to work.

beige book   An important Federal Reserve anecdotal report on various economic conditions from each of the District banks. It contains interviews with key business leaders, economists, and other sources. The beige book is so called because it comes in a beige-colored cover. It is published for internal Federal Reserve purposes and is issued eight times a year.

beneficiary   The person who is named in a benefit or insurance plan to receive specified money if the employee dies. It is recommended that you review the beneficiaries of your benefits if you have a change in your life situation, such as a divorce.

bequest   A gift of personal property through a will. This is in contrast to devise, which is a gift of real property, namely real estate.

Best Insurance Report   Best Insurance Reports rate health and life insurance companies. The highest rating, an A++, is only given to a little over 10 percent of all companies. You can find Best Insurance Reports in your library, or call BestLine at (900) 420-0400 ($2.50 per minute).

bid and asked   The price a willing buyer will pay (bid) and the price a willing seller wants (ask).

Big Bang   A monumental day for London's financial markets, October 27, 1986, when it opened up to foreign firms. See May Day.

big board   A casual term for the New York Stock Exchange (NYSE).

big uglies   Stocks that are out of favor with the investing public, usually large industrial companies such as steel or chemical firms that are not in glamorous businesses. Because they are unpopular, Big Uglies typically sell at low price/earnings and price/book value ratios.

binder   An agreement by an insurance agent to immediately cover property such as a house even before an actual insurance policy is issued.

blow off   Very strong, almost frenzied, stock market buying, propelling the market to new highs, which will probably be corrected in the future.

blowout The instant sale of an initial stock offering, because of a strong demand for it.

blue chip A stock of very high quality. Usually considered a lower risk stock because it is from a large, established, and consistently profitable corporation. Companies like GE, Exxon, and Ford are examples of blue chip companies.

blue sky laws State regulation of the offering and sale of securities within the state. The term is derived from investors' buying something worthless, like a piece of the blue sky. States hope that these laws limit the amount of securities that are without value.

Bo Derek stock A perfect stock with an exemplary record of earning growth, product quality and stock price appreciation. These stocks are named after the movie "10" in which Bo Derek was depicted as the perfect woman.

boiler-room operation An illegal operation selling small-cap stocks that are thinly traded, and therefore sensitive to market fluctuations. A bank of phones is set-up with telemarketers pushing specific small stocks and thereby pushing the prices of those stocks artificially high. The operators then sell their own stock, making a profit, before the prices fall back down to realistic levels.

bond A long-term liability of a company, municipality, or government, usually specified by a specific interest rate (coupon rate) and for a specific length of time (maturity). It is essentially a loan made by investors to the organization. The investors earn interest while the corporation or government gets the cash it needs for major projects. Corporate bonds are usually sold in units of $1,000, municipals in $5,000, and Treasury notes and bonds can be of different denominations. A zero coupon bond pays no interest but the initial value is greatly reduced, increasing in value to the date of maturity where it equals the full value of the bond.

bond fund A mutual fund of bonds, either only of a specific type, like long-term treasury bonds, or some mixture of corporate and treasury bonds, usually of similar maturity rates.

bonus A lump-sum payment for work well done. It can be paid to selected employees or to an entire department.

book value A company's worth if all its assets were sold and its debts were paid off, sometimes referred to as net book value. The value at which assets are carried on the balance sheet. That is, book value is the cost of the asset less any accumulated depreciation or amortization. Book value is based on historical cost of assets and may vary significantly from market value.

bottom fishing The buying of low priced out-of-fashion stocks that are hoped-for bargains.

boutique Small, specialized brokerage firm that deals with a limited clientele and offers a limited product line. A highly regarded securities analyst may form a research boutique which clients use as a resource for buying and selling certain stocks. A boutique is the opposite of a financial supermarket which offers a wide variety of services to a wide variety of clients.

broker An agent who arranges for the buying and selling of investments. A full-service broker will give advice on your investments besides carrying out transactions and charging you a higher commission for the service. A discount broker will place your buy or sell order generally with little or no advice, thus charging lower commissions than the full-service broker. A deep-discount broker offers the cheapest service of all, but usually just for investors who trade in large amounts or very frequently.

broker commission See commission.

broker dealer (BD) See dealer.

bucket shop The illegal activity of taking orders to buy or sell but either never executing the orders or executing them only when it is advantageous to the broker.

budget A plan for annual expenditures and revenues. Individuals, businesses, and governments set an annual budget as a basis for spending with a projection of revenue. A balanced budget is being proposed for many of the developed countries, including the United States.

bull; bull market A market characterized by rising prices, or an investor who expects the market to rise and invests that way.

burnout A general term for an employee, usually in a stressful job, who has a decrease in energy and motivation for a job. This can be temporary for individuals such as nurses or therapists who deal with personal stresses of others on a daily basis. It can also refer to an employee who becomes frustrated after doing the same job for a number of years and needs a respite.

business cycle A recurring period of increased business activity with a slowdown occurring after a number of years. Traditionally there are four periods of the cycle: expansion, prosperity, contraction, and recession. Since World War II, the business cycle occurred from three to five years in the United States. In the 1980s, the business cycle lasted about eight years, and it seems that perhaps it might be duplicating that in the 1990s.

business risk   There are several risks that investors consider: market risk, inflation risk, and business risk. Business risk is the risk that a business faces within its industry. A business that is well-positioned within its industry has a greater market share (and, perhaps, proprietary products) and has a lower business risk than one that is not well-positioned.

buy-and-hold strategy   An investment approach of buying high-quality stocks and then holding them for many years. Since good solid stocks should continue to grow, this is a realistic and generally sound strategy.

cafeteria plan   Employee options that allow an employer to take money out of a paycheck for things like retirement plans, insurance, and day care. Just like in a cafeteria, employees are allowed those options they wish to pay for. The money taken out reduces your taxable income. These are sometimes called salary reduction plans.

call option   An option to buy a stock at a specified price. The two kinds of options are put and call. A call option is a right to buy.

callable bond   A bond that can be called before its maturity date, typically five to ten years from the issue date. Treasury notes and bonds are generally not callable. Companies and municipalities call bonds early to reissue them at lower interest rates, saving considerable amounts of money. This only happens when interest rates decline. Investors think they will be getting high interest until maturity, only to be surprised and disappointed when bonds are called.

cancellation   The termination of any insurance policy.

capital   1. Money, or, in economic theory, assets capable of producing income which is more broadly defined than money. It can mean physical capital like machinery, equipment or factories, in addition to money, investments, or securities. 2. Owner's equity in a company. That is, the amount of funds that the owners invested in the company.

capital expenditures   The amount spent for long-term productive assets.

capital gains and losses   The profit, or loss, made on an investment. The selling price minus the tax basis equals the amount of capital gains, or losses. If the investments or property was owned for over one year, then it is a long-term capital gain or loss. If shorter, then a short-term capital gain or loss. If you have several gains and losses during the year, you follow this saying: Net your longs, net your shorts, net your nets. The result is the amount of gains or losses you can take on your taxes. There are limits on the amount of capital losses that can be taken each year.

capital improvements Improvements made to a company's main long-term assets, such as plants and buildings.

capital markets Stock and bond markets where longer term securities are traded, such as the New York Stock Exchange. This is in contrast to short-term markets such as commercial paper and treasury bills, called the money market.

capitalization The term capitalization, often shortened to cap, refers to multiplying the number of shares of stock times the price of shares. This is called the company's capitalization. It indicates how large or small the company is relative to other companies. It is a quick and meaningful measurement. Capitalization may also refer to the amount and type of longer-term debt of a company, such as long-term bonds, common stock, and preferred stock.

capital market The financial markets for investments. Businesses raise capital by selling securities, stocks, and bonds, and individuals buy investments as a means of income, savings, and growth for their future wealth.

capital stock The total amount of physical capital in an economy, such as equipment, machinery, or factories.

capitalism An economic system based on the principles of free competition, private ownership, and profit maximization. Individuals own the means of production. This is in contrast to socialism, in which everyone in society owns the means of production of all goods and services.

cartel A cartel is formed when independent companies group together to agree on trade restrictions.

cash 1. Another name for money market instruments or money market funds. Used when an investor does not know in what to invest. Some interest is earned in these short-term safe securities, like T-bills. Sometimes referred to as a parking place or a holding place, until an attractive investment is found. 2. Currency, bank accounts, and other "near-cash" instruments that are very liquid and can easily be converted to cash.

cash accounting; cash basis A basic method of accounting in which revenue and expenses are recorded only when money is received or paid out. This is in contrast to accrual accounting in which revenue and expenses are recorded when earned or incurred.

cash budget A projected schedule of cash receipts and expenses over a given period of time.

cash cow   Business that generates a continuing flow of cash. Such a business usually has well-established brand names whose family stimulates repeated buying of the products. Stocks that are cash cows have dependable dividends.

cash flow   The amount of cash generated from a particular business activity or project.

cash surrender value   The amount of money a life-insurance policy holder would receive if they were to stop the insurance and take whatever value is in the policy.

cash value   The amount of money in a whole life-insurance policy that can be withdrawn while still keeping the policy in force.

casualty; casualty insurance; casualty loss Casualty insurance covers unexpected losses, called casualty losses, due to an accident, fire, catastrophe, or company negligence. These unfortunate events are called casualty losses.

catastrophic   medical coverage A form of medical insurance that provides significant payments for very costly medical conditions. It is considered the most critical type of insurance, because it is unlikely that an individual would have enough money to cover these costly bills. This form of payment is usually built in to major medical or general medical coverage.

CATS   A trademarked security, originated by Salomon Brothers and Bache, which stands for Certificate of Accrual on Treasury Securities. It involves taking apart treasury securities and selling pieces to investors. A number of these treasury dissections have been performed by the major brokerage houses and each has a trademark name.

CD (Certificate of deposit)   A popular bank interest investment, usually with a maturity of six months to five years. Primarily used by conservative investors.

central bank   The bank that functions as the governmental bank that controls and regulates banks, banking, and the money supply in a country, and coordinates international matters with other central banks. The Federal Reserve Bank is that official bank in the United States. In France, it's the Bank of France, in Germany, it's the Bundesbank, and in Canada, it's the Bank of Canada.

certificates   In the world of stock market investments, the stock certificate is the actual piece of paper with all the special information about the stock, such as the issuer and the number of shares the certificate represents. A bond certificate is the record of your investment.

Certified Financial Planner (CFP)   The main certification of financial planners who have met certain requirements of knowledge and experience in investments, insurance, taxes, and financial calculations.

certified public accountant (CPA)   One who has passed the CPA exams and met the state statutory requirements to practice accounting in that state. Only those who meet these requirements are able to use the initials CPA. A CPA audits the books of a company and gives an expression of the accuracy of the company's financial statements.

Chartered Financial Analyst (CFA)   A financial analyst who has met certain requirements of knowledge and experience in economics, security analysis, portfolio management, and financial accounting.

Chicago Board of Trade (CBT)   Established in 1848, it was first an exchange to trade forward grain contracts, but now trades in many futures and options.

Chicago Board Options Exchange (COBE)   The first organized trading exchange for options, established in 1973.

Chicago Mercantile Exchange (CME)   Started in 1919, it is an exchange trading in many agricultural commodities.

Chicago school   Milton Friedman and other economists who either taught at the University of Chicago or who promote the ideas of macroeconomics, monetarism, and free markets.

chief financial officer (CFO)   The senior company officer in charge of all accounting and financial reporting, usually reporting directly to the president of the company.

Chinese wall   Imaginary barrier between the investment banking, corporate finance and research departments of a brokerage house and the sales and trading departments. Since the investment banking side has sensitive knowledge of impending deals such as takeovers, new stock and bond issues, divestitures, spinoffs and the like, it would be unfair to the general investment public if the sales and trading side of the firm had advance knowledge of such transactions. So several SEC and stock exchange rules mandate that a Chinese Wall be erected to prevent premature leakage of this market-moving information. It became law with the passage of SEC Rule 10b-5 of the Securities Exchange Act of 1934. The investment banking department uses code names and logs of the people who have access to key information in an attempt to keep the identities of the parties secret until the deal is publicly announced.

churn; churning   The unethical, and illegal, activity by a broker to over actively trade an account so as to increase brokerage commissions instead of trying to increase the profit of the account.

circuit breakers   Official halting of trading to cool down markets, just like electricity that is stopped by fuses or circuit breakers when overheating. If and when markets plunge, the circuit breaker means that the stock exchange could stop the trading for several hours, or even for a day. These rules started in 1988, after an assessment of the 508-point plunge in the Dow Jones industrial average (a 22.6 percent drop) on October 19, 1987. The rule was established to stop the trading if the market drops 250 points, and then again if it drops 400 points for the day.

claim   A request made by an insured party for payment from the insurance company.

Class A stock   The name given to the basic class of stock when there is another class. This indicates that there are some differences between the rights of the stockholders in each class. The other class of stock is usually called Class B stock.

classes of stock   Shares of stock allow for four general rights: voting at stockholders' meetings, a share of earnings, a share in the distribution if company is liquidated, and to subscribe to any additional issues of the stock held. This last right is known as a preemptive right. There can be one class of stock or more. If more, then each class may have more or less of the four general rights. "Common" stock is one basic form of stock, "preferred" another. There can be Class A and Class B stock, each having prescribed rights.

classical economics   The economic school of thought that emphasized free markets, competition, and small government. Economists Adam Smith, David Ricardo, and Alfred Marshall were of this school.

clearing house   A firm that facilitates the execution of trades by an exchange by transferring funds, providing delivery of certificates, and guaranteeing the performance of trading obligations.

closed-end fund; closed-end investment company   A type of mutual fund with a fixed number of shares. Not as common as regular or open-end mutual funds. They are traded on the stock exchanges or over-the-counter. Closed-end funds are more like regular stocks than their counterpart, open-end funds.

closing   A meeting with buyer and seller, as well as any attorneys and bankers involved in the sale of a piece of real estate, at which the final transactions take place. After the closing, the buyer takes possession of the property and the seller gets all of the net sales proceeds. Not to be confused with the contract signing. Note that closing is a noun, but you may use the verb "close" to talk about the meeting.

closing costs   There are a number of costs associated with a closing—you don't put all those people in a room for free. The closing costs include items like transaction fees, attorney fees, and other bank, insurance, and government (recording) fees. Many banks estimate your closing costs for you when you apply for a mortgage so that you can plan for them.

closing statement   That document detailing all items that have to be satisfied before the real estate transaction can take place, such as fees and taxes to be paid.

COBRA (Consolidated Omnibus Budget Reconciliation Act of 1985)   One of the longest and most difficult titles of legislation, but one that is of significant practical use, if you lose your job. You can continue to be covered under the company's medical plan for up to eighteen months by paying roughly the same as what it costs the company. Actually, the law says that there are several "qualifying events" that will allow you to do this, which includes termination, reduced work hours, death, and divorce.

coinsurance   A benefits practice that requires the employee to pay for a portion of the benefit, such as medical insurance for which the employee must either make a small co-payment (usually in the amount of $5 to $20) per doctor's visit or pay, for instance, 20 percent of the entire bill.

collateral   Any asset you offer as a guarantee that you will repay a loan.

Collateralized Mortgage Obligations (CMOs)   A security offered by the Federal Home Loan Mortgage Corporation that provides a pass-through of mortgage principal and interest to investors.

collection agency   The outside firm given accounts receivable that have not been collected in an attempt to recover some, if not all, of the outstanding payments.

collision   Sudden damage to a vehicle due to an accident.

commercial paper   A short-term note issued by companies. The length of issue is usually from thirty to 270 days.

commission   A compensation-based practice of paying a salesperson a percentage of the sales for the month, or other period. Wall Street brokers and insurance agents are often paid by this method as well; a percentage of their sales is the salesperson's gain. Thus, the more you sell, the greater your compensation.

commitment   A promise by a bank or lending institution that you will get a loan at a specified amount and interest rate. The bank's commitment is usually for a short time.

commodity An article of trade or commerce, usually an agricultural or mining product. Sugar, wheat, soybeans, and gasoline are examples of commodities.

commodity currency Currency made of either gold or silver, or that can be exchanged for gold or silver. Today, the United States does not have a commodity currency; its money cannot be traded for gold or silver.

common stock The shares of a company having voting rights and a share of earnings when dividends are declared.

communism An extreme socialist economic system based on the ownership of production by society, communism requires that the government plan and control the economy. In practice, communism, like socialism, is a system where the government owns most of the key industries and controls prices and the supply of goods and services. This system is the opposite of capitalism, in which individuals own the means of production.

company contributions Refers to the payment made into a pension or 401(k)-type savings plan by the company. This is over and above your own contributions. The usual company contribution to a 401(k) plan is 50 percent of your contributions up to 6 percent of your pay. Thus, you make 50 percent on your money for just being there, as an employee.

competition The tension between similar businesses to keep prices down and productivity up. The consumer benefits from reasonable prices for products and services. Perfect competition, as opposed to imperfect competition, or monopoly, is an economic term that describes how competition is ideally supposed to work in an ideal capitalist society.

comptroller An older spelling of controller. See controller.

consignment When a company or individual places goods in a store but retains title to the goods. If the goods are not sold, the owner, not the store, is responsible for them.

consolidated statement; consolidated financial statements The combining of all business units of a company into one overall set of financial statements.

conspicuous consumption Ostentatious buying of goods in order to impress others. A term used by American economist Thorstein Veblen in his 1899 book The Theory of the Leisure Class.

constant dollars The value of the dollar in a base year. If 1990 is chosen as the base for constant dollars, any inflation or decrease in the value of the dollar after that year is adjusted so all actual purchasing power can be compared to that year.

consumer   The buyer of goods and services. The hypothetical person that economists study.

consumer confidence   A measure of how typical consumers feel about their current situation and their faith in the future. If people feel good about where they are and where they're going, consumer confidence is said to be high, and the economy will benefit. Even during an economic recovery, if consumers don't have confidence, they will be hesitant to spend. Consumer confidence surveys generally check a number of different things: how people feel about their job security, whether they would buy big-ticket items, and whether they will spend consistently on short term purchases.

consumer goods   Manufactured products used by consumers, not businesses. Durable goods are those that usually have a useful life of three years or more, like cars and refrigerators. Non-durable goods, like toys or games, which we know don't last very long, are generally consumed, or used, right away.

consumer price index (CPI)   A monthly measure of price movements by the Bureau of Labor Statistics. A "basket of goods" is constructed of food, shelter, clothing, medical care, entertainment, and other expenditures, then priced each month. However, the basket of goods is fixed, so consumer habits are not measured, only fixed prices. Although it roughly measures the cost of living, the CPI doesn't take into consideration factors such as consumers buying more rice if the price of potatoes increases. The fixed basket of goods is updated from time to time. It is used to adjust Social Security payments and other government benefits that have cost-of-living increases built in.

consumer spending; consumption   What economists call buying goods or purchasing services. Some products, like foods, are literally consumed, while others, like toys, are just used. Economists consider both to be examples of consumption.

consumption function   Ratio of how much people consume to how much they earn. All things being equal, it is generally assumed that consumption will increase if income increases. More specifically, as income rises, savings rise, along with spending. As income decreases, savings decrease, along with spending.

contingency; contingency reserve   An event that may occur for which a company desires, or is forced, to set aside funds. For example, if a company has a pending lawsuit, it may create a contingency reserve for any future damages it may need to pay.

contingent beneficiary   A second person who will be beneficiary of an insurance policy if the main beneficiary is not alive.

contract   In real estate, the buyer and seller sign a contract that commits the two of them to go through with the deal. The actual closing, when they transfer possession of the property, usually takes place a month or two later.

contrarian   An investor who is going against popular momentum or opinions. When most investors are buying, a contrarian may be selling, and vice versa.

convertibles   Securities that are a cross between bonds and stocks. Like a bond, it offers a fixed rate of return, but it also can be converted to the company's stock by a specific date. Convertibles can offer the best of both worlds in that they pay more than a stock in income and if the stock rises then the investor can buy the stock and participate in that rise.

co-payment   A term applied to health insurance where you pay a percentage of the medical costs, for instance 20 percent, and your company pays the other percentage, 80 percent.

corporate culture   The attitudes and beliefs that guide daily behavior at a company, or in the corporate world in general. Some companies encourage casualness to the point where beards, jeans, and pizza parties are the norm.

corporate-owned life insurance   A somewhat complicated cash-value life-insurance arrangement between a company and its executives. The company typically pays the premiums, holds the policy, and receives the death benefit when the employee dies.

corporate welfare   Payments to businesses either in the form of a subsidy, like farming subsidies, or tax relief for special purposes such as a research and development tax credit.

correction   A term investors don't like to hear. It is a downturn in the market after a run-up in prices. Usually considered a normal adjustment to a more realistic level of prices after the market has moved upward with considerable momentum.

cost   The expenditure of funds for specific financial needs of a company, such as equipment, salaries, investments, or general expenses. Cost is a term used in many contexts of a company's finances, such as fixed, variable, marginal, historical or replacement.

cost accounting   Accounting methods used to provide internal cost information for managerial analysis and decisions. This is in contrast to financial accounting, which provides information for external uses, such as bankers, investors, and regulators.

cost-benefit analysis   An appraisal of all social as well as economic aspects of a business project or a government policy.

cost containment   Efforts by a company to reduce, or at least hold down, rising medical costs.

costs of goods sold   The costs of materials used in the products and goods that a company makes.

cost of living adjustment (COLA)   An automatic increase due to inflation or some other index. Currently Social Security is adjusted annually by a COLA, specifically by the increase in inflation as measured by the CPI (consumer price index).

cost-push inflation   The increase in inflation due to increased costs of production. Increased labor costs or raw materials, like the oil crisis of the 1970s, are said to be pushed from the cost side. This is in contrast to demand-pull, where the demand has increased from consumers, thus pulling up prices.

cost shifting   Transferring more of the costs of medical insurance to the employees, in hopes that employees will exercise more discretion with optional health costs.

Council of Economic Advisers   A group of economists officially advising the President of the United States on economic matters. It was established in 1946.

coupon; coupon rate   A bond's interest rate. Bearer bonds used to have coupons attached, which the investor would cut out to redeem.

coverage   Can refer to being included in certain benefits of the company, such as a medical or a 401(k) plan, or the scope of what is covered by an insurance policy. It can also refer to having enough people in the office at any one time to make sure the phones are "covered."

covering the short position   Selling short is a way to make money in the stock market when stocks go down. You borrow stocks to first sell them, then buy the same stocks, which sounds either contorted or illegal. It is neither. If the price drops, as you hoped, you buy the stocks back at the lower price, return them, and keep the profit (minus a commission, of course). When you actually buy the stocks, you are "covering the short position."

CPI (consumer price index)   See consumer price index.

crash A sudden collapse in the value of stocks.

creative accounting A mostly casual term, which refers to manipulating numbers to fit the results a company wants (within the rules of accounting, of course).

credit 1. A system that gives the consumer the right to use goods or services without immediately having to pay for them. 2. In accounting lingo, it refers to the entries on the right side of the accounts, you know, debits on the left and credits on the right.

credit card A method of purchasing an item and paying for it later. The bank issuing the card will usually give a limit to the amount you are able to charge.

credit crunch or squeeze Governmental restrictions on bank credit or the pull-back of businesses offering credit.

credit report A report from an independent company of the borrower's credit history—how much outstanding credit and debt the borrower is carrying and how promptly payments were made.

credit scoring Objective methodology used by credit grantors to determine how much, if any, credit to grant to an applicant. Credit scoring is devised by three different methods: by a third-party firm, by the credit grantor, or by the credit in cooperation with the credit grantor. Some of the most common factors in scoring are income, assets, length of living in one place and past record of using credit. Any negative events in the past, such as bankruptcies or tax delinquencies, will sharply reduce an applicant's credit score.

credit terms The conditions specified by the bank for the money borrowed by a company, such as the amount of available credit, the percentage rate of interest, and when the funds are due to be paid.

credit union A company bank, sort of, that pays usually a slightly higher amount of interest for deposits and charges slightly lower interest rates for loans. It is a chartered bank that has as its depositors and borrowers employees of a particular company only. Payroll deductions into savings plans are usually allowed.

creditor One who is owed money, versus the debtor who owes it.

cumulative dividends Dividends on designated preferred stock that have not been paid, but will be paid, when available, to the preferred stock holders before the common stock holders. Also known as accumulated dividends and dividends in arrears.

currency Simply another word for money, paper or coin.

current assets Short-term assets of a company, such as cash or notes that are expected to be used or converted to cash within one year.

current liabilities Short-term liabilities of a company, such as accounts payable or loans that are expected to be paid to the company within one year.

current ratio A ratio calculated by taking the current assets and dividing by the current liabilities. It measures how well a company can meet its short-term obligations.

current value A value of an asset that is determined to be generally at a true market value. Other terms that may be used interchangeably are replacement value, market value or fair market value, and present value. This is in contrast to historical cost, which is the original cost of the asset.

current yield The current income of a bond or stock, either through interest or dividends.

CUSIP number The security identification number that is assigned to each stock certificate. It stands for Committee on Uniform Securities Identification Procedures.

cyclical stocks Stocks which follow the general business cycle, going up at the beginning of the cycle and falling during a recession. Airlines typically have cyclical stocks: When the economy is floundering, people don't travel as much.

damages The injury or financial loss suffered by a person, giving rise to an insurance claim.

day order Placing an order to buy or sell a security that will expire at the end of the day. An investor may wish to reconsider the transaction the next day, thus wants to control the trade on a day-by-day basis.

day trader An active investor who speculates on short-term trades, often in and out of a security within a day.

dead cat bounce Sharp rise in stock prices after a severe decline. The saying refers to the fact that a dead cat dropped from a high place will bounce. Often the bounce is a result of short-sellers covering their positions at a profit.

dealers Individuals or firms that buy and sell stocks for themselves rather than for someone else. This is in contrast to brokers, who buy and sell for others. Broker-dealers do both.

death benefit A general term referring to any one of several payments because of the death of a person. It could be a life-insurance payment, a pension payment, or just a lump sum paid by a company to a beneficiary.

debenture A type of corporate bond that doesn't have specific assets pledged to it. They are issued based on the strength of the issuer's credit.

debit In accounting lingo, an entry made on the asset or expense side of a ledger or account, or in bookkeeping, used to denote the left side of the ledger. It is the obligations of a company, short-term and long-term, like accounts payable.

debit card A debit card is very different from a credit card by deducting the amount of your purchase directly from your banking account. Whereas you have a time lag with a credit card to receive the bill and then pay it, no such time is involved with a debit card. You must have enough in your account to cover what you buy.

debt 1. The amount of money that a person, business, or government owes. In 1996 the U.S. Government debt was about $5 trillion. That is, the total of all U.S. Treasury securities equals that amount and will have to eventually be repaid (although new debt could replace it). To put it in personal terms, think of it as the government's credit card balance. This is in contrast to the deficit, which is the amount of money added to (or subtracted from) the debt each year. 2. One of the two basic methods of raising capital for a company, by bonds, called debt securities. See equity.

debt securities Investments, like bonds, in which the company or government borrows money from investors to finance long-term projects.

debt service Interest on loans along with any payments on the principal currently due.

debt limit The official amount of government debt that is allowed. The Congress sets that limit and inevitably increases it as the need for additional deficit spending occurs.

decelerate To slow down. By most predictions, after a number of years a sustained economy will tend to decelerate. It will be signaled by a downswing in the leading economic indicators.

dedicate; dedication Designing an investment portfolio to provide the needed income or principal at some future time when specific liabilities are expected to occur. Pension funds estimate when and how much money they will need for retirements, then plan a portfolio that will provide the necessary money to coincide with those expected payments.

deductible The amount an individual is liable to pay; any amount above the deductible is paid for by the insurer.

deductions Subtractions allowed from your adjusted gross income. All taxpayers are entitled to a standard deduction; if you have certain expenses that exceed that amount you can take them against your adjusted gross income. This reduces your taxable income and, thus, you pay less taxes. These expenses are mortgage interest payments (not the part of the mortgage that repays the principal), real estate taxes, certain medical expenses, and charity donations, among others.

deed A written document that conveys any sort of interest in real estate.

deep in/out of the money An option in which the strike price is far above/below the price of the market price of the security. In other words, at the moment you've done either very well or very poorly.

deep-discount broker A large investor may use a deep-discount broker. These brokers offer greatly reduced commissions to those who buy frequently and/or who buy in large amounts.

default The failure to make a payment when due. The term generally refers to a company that is unable to meet many of its financial obligations.

deferred annuity An annuity that is anticipated to be paid some time in the future, as opposed to an immediate annuity.

deferred compensation Salary or bonuses that are not paid during the year in which they are earned, but later, usually after retirement.

deficit Excess of expenses over revenues. When the government spends more money than it takes in through taxes and fees, then it has a deficit and has to borrow more money.

deficit financing The borrowing of money by a government to pay for expenditures that exceed taxation revenues. The U.S. Government issues additional Treasury securities to finance deficits.

deficit spending Any spending by the government that exceeds what it takes in as revenues.

defined benefit plan A traditional pension plan where the benefit is "defined" by a formula, and often based on the last final years of employment.

defined-contribution plan The most popular investment and retirement plan in recent years, such as 401(k) plans. They can also be a tax-deferred annuity or 403(b) plan. It is the amount of "contribution" that is defined, not the ultimate benefit as in a defined benefit plan. The final benefit will depend on how well the investments do, which depends on which investments are selected.

deflation A decline in prices; the opposite of inflation. It's unusual to have a sustained period of deflation. Our experience since World War II has been one of steady inflation with spurts of higher inflation, but not deflation. The Great Depression saw actual deflation. See disinflation.

defraud To deprive a person or company of property or rights through some means of deceit.

demand Our desire for specific products and services, tempered by our ability to pay for them. Thus our demand for goods depends on the desirability and price of them. This is one side of supply and demand. The supply side is the production of the goods.

demand-pull The increase in prices due to an increase in consumer demand for products or services, thereby pulling up prices. This is in contrast to cost-push pressure of increased labor costs or raw materials, the cost side, to increase prices.

demand-side economics The economic philosophy that emphasizes the demand for goods and services, often by government spending, to stimulate economic growth. See supply-side economics.

dental coverage Some insurance coverage for dental work, such as annual checkups, filling of cavities, or more serious work. Usually there is a deductible, meaning you pay a portion while the company pays the rest.

dependents Generally, your children and yourself and spouse. You are able to reduce your taxable income for each dependent, thus lowering your taxes. Sometimes others who depend on you for support can be included, such as relatives or elderly parents.

depletion The loss of a natural resource as it is used up, such as coal, timber, oil, or gas. Accountants assign a cost of that loss and record it in the accounts and financial statements of the company.

depreciation 1. The reduction in value of assets, usually in yearly terms. Governments allow businesses to deduct on their taxes the decreased value of its plant and equipment. 2. An accounting method of spreading the cost of an asset over its useful life. Thus, the cost of expensive new equipment doesn't adversely affect any one year's financial statements. Depreciation can be seen as the loss of value of an asset over time, and the financial statements reflect this in some way year-by-year.

depression A significant and prolonged downturn in the economy. The Great Depression of the 1930s was such an event, resulting in extremely high unemployment (estimated as high as 25 percent), along with low wages and declining prices. A related economic term is recession, which is a mild form of an economic downturn. An economy is said to be in recession after two consecutive quarters of decreasing gross domestic product.

deregulation A process of removing government regulation on a certain industry. The idea of deregulation is to let the market determine prices and supply.

derivatives An investment is a step removed from the actual security. It is said that a derivative is "derived" from another security, or form of investment such as a commodity. It is typically an option, but can be other sophisticated derived securities. For example, rather than investing in oil directly, you can bet on the way the oil prices will go through an option. Because they are often difficult to grasp, investors, including sophisticated companies, frequently lose money when they invest in derivatives.

designated order turnaround (DOT) A DOT is a computerized system designed to handle smaller orders of fewer than 1,200 shares on the Stock Exchange. A majority of trades are handled by the DOT, or designated order turnaround, system.

devaluation The reduction in the value of one currency in relation to another. This is a somewhat dramatic event under exchange rates that are fixed, but with floating rates, weekly and daily fluctuations can occur.

diminishing returns The law stating that, after a certain point, adding more people or machinery to the production process will not yield a proportionate amount of greater returns.

direct cost; direct labor; direct material Costs that can be directly identified and traced to specific activities such as labor, materials, or manufacturing.

direct investments An investment term referring to investing directly into a business through ownership or near-ownership. This could be owning, say, 25 percent of a business, or buying a limited partnership, which is ownership without management responsibility.

direct rollover The preferred employee method to put a benefit plan distribution into a rollover IRA, such as when an employee leaves a company and gets a lump-sum distribution from their 401(k) plan. This method allows for the money to go from the 401(k) directly into a new, or existing, IRA. The non-preferred method is taking the lump sum and within sixty days putting it into a Rollover IRA, however, the company must then withhold 20 percent of the distribution! Thus, it could cause a major immediate tax bite.

disability Not being able to work due to illness or an accident. Companies usually have a short-term disability policy that may pay your salary, or part of it, for a certain period of time. Often, it is tied to how long you've been an employee. For longer disabilities, usually over six months, companies may have a long-term disability insurance program. Social Security also covers long-term disability, but it must be a severe case.

disability insurance Insurance that covers one's salary in case a disability prevents an individual from working.

disbursement The payment of a bill.

discount broker A broker who primarily buys and sells securities, as opposed to a full-service broker who also provides investment advice.

discount rate One of two interest rates that is controlled by the Federal Reserve. The discount rate is the rate that the Federal Reserve charges member banks to borrow money. See federal funds rate.

discounted cash flow The present value of a series of cash flows. It calculates the current value of future payments or income, or both.

discretionary account An account at a brokerage firm where the investor has allowed the broker full discretion as to what securities to buy and sell and when.

discretionary cost A cost that can be varied by a manager or a business unit, such as the costs of business travel and meals, training, or charitable giving.

disinflation The reduction or even elimination of inflation. Disinflation is thus a stabilization of inflation at a low percentage, whereas deflation is a negative inflation. See deflation.

disposable income The available money consumers have after income taxes. It is the money consumers can spend on goods and services or put toward savings.

distributions The profits a company makes that are dispersed to its investors, such as dividends. It also pertains to mutual fund dividends and capital gains that are dispersed or charged to its investors.

diversification A fancy name for the saying "Don't put all your eggs in one basket." More technically it means investing in stocks and bonds through an asset allocation strategy.

dividend reinvestment plan (DRIP) A plan that allows stockholders to automatically reinvest their dividends in additional shares of the company. To encourage stockholders to purchase additional shares in this way, the company usually does not charge a fee for this service.

dividends   The payment to stockholders of a portion of the earnings of the company. Dividends are usually paid by established companies, in contrast to a new company, which will often reinvest its earnings to grow the business.

dollar   Our currency, which is used in financial and business markets around the world.

dollar-cost averaging   A popular mutual fund strategy of investing a set amount of money each month to average the price at which the fund is bought. If the price has dropped, then more shares will be bought, and if the price has risen, less shares are bought. A lower price is considered a good purchase because the investor may believe it will rise in the future. Thus the investor has bought more shares at lower prices, for a desired increased future return.

double-entry accounting   The common accounting system of two entries for each item, that is, a debit (on the left) and a credit (on the right). As an example, when your company pays your salary, it is entered as an increase in salary expense (debit) and a decrease in available cash (credit).

Dow Jones Industrial Average (DJIA)   Referred to as "The Dow," this is the most widely referred-to market indicator. It is computed by adding the stock prices of thirty major industrial companies and dividing that number by a factor that adjusts for any distortions. When a news show reports that the market has fallen by ten points, it is referring to the Dow Jones Industrial Average.

Dow theory   In 1884 Charles Dow used the closing prices of eleven stocks to represent the stock market and later with Eddie Jones established the Wall Street Journal. The original eleven stocks were comprised of nine railroads and two industrial companies. On December 19, 1900 he stated what was to become the Dow theory: That there were three movements going on in the market at the same time—day-to-day movements, short swings of two weeks to a month, and the main movements, lasting about four years.

downgrade   When a rating service drops the rating of a company.

downsizing   Reducing the number of employees and specifically rearranging who does what in a department, or company.

dual listing   A security being traded, listed, on more than one exchange, such as on the New York Stock Exchange and a regional exchange such as the Midwest exchange.

due diligence   The investigation and analysis of an investment by a financial planner, or other financial advisor, as to the soundness and appropriateness of an investment for an investor. The planner looks for such things as economic value, security law violations, accurate accounting projections, and the promoter's experience and track record.

Dun & Bradstreet reports   A published source of credit information about companies. The information includes a credit history, any legal proceedings, current debts, and any other useful financial information.

durable goods   Manufactured goods that are generally considered to last over three years such as cars, refrigerators, and furniture. See consumer goods.

duration   A measurement of a bond's sensitivity to changes in interest rates. It is a mathematical calculation of the weighted average present value of the bond's stream of payments. If a bond has a duration of ten, then a one percent increase or decrease in interest rates will change the value 10 percent in the opposite direction. For instance, if interest rates increase one percent, a bond with a duration of ten will decrease 10 percent in value.

EAFE (Europe, Australia, Far East)   An index of the major markets outside of the U.S. by Morgan Stanley, an investment banking firm. It is comprised of about 1,000 individual stocks.

earned income   Income you get the old fashioned way—you earn it. Often called earnings. This is in contrast to investment income, such as interest, which is often referred to as unearned income.

earnest money   Up-front money to show seriousness in buying property.

earnings per share; earnings ratio   A calculation taking the net income for the year divided by the average number of shares outstanding. It is generally an indication of the amount of retained earnings that are available for dividends or reinvestment projects.

easement   Permission to use a portion of someone else's property without owning it. Towns, for example, have easements that allow them to install underground lines through private property.

easy or loose money   The monetary policy of the Federal Reserve (Fed) to make more money available, usually in hopes of stimulating the economy. This is the opposite of the Fed's policy of tight money, which is used to try to slow down the economy.

econometrics   Math and statistical methods in the study of economics. Usually involved in the creation of mathematical models to describe and then predict how the economy would respond given specific actions, either by companies or governments or both.

economic expansion or growth The expansion or growth over a number of years of the economy's ability to produce goods and services.

economic indicators Data, ratios, or other figures that not only describe the economy, but tend to forecast the direction of it as well. The leading indicators use information about the number of housing starts or the amount of business inventories to describe the health of the economy today and to project the short-term future of the economy.

economic life The length of time an asset is estimated to be useful, such as computers, buildings, or machinery.

economic model A theoretical mathematical or statistical relation of economic variables. Models can be simple, for example, if inflation increases, then interest rates increase. Models can also be quite complex with numerous equations and hundreds of variables.

economics The study of a society's production of goods and services and their distribution and consumption. Some of the specific subjects studied by economists are how markets work, how prices and demand are related, and how to deal with problems of inflation, unemployment, and competition. Economists also examine how actions of governments affect the economy, such as taxation, deficit spending, and regulation, as well as how countries deal with each other in foreign trade and the balance of payments. Economics is said to provide the theories for the optimization of available resources. It has also been said that economics is the "dismal science" (by the English historian Thomas Carlyle in the 1800s).

economy The business activity of a country or region.

EE bonds U.S. savings bonds that accumulate interest until cashed in. This is contrast to HH bonds that pay out interest semi-annually just like a regular bond.

efficient market Economists refer to an efficient market as one that is analyzed thoroughly and everyone has lots of information available about it.

electronic filing The ability to file your taxes electronically, through computers. There are probably several providers locally for you that are set up with the IRS to do this.

electronic transfer When money is debited and credited from one account to another account without actually physically passing through anyone's hands.

embezzlement The illegal taking of property by someone entrusted with its possession, such as a bank employee's taking money from the till.

emerging markets Countries that are growing up economically.

employee benefits The cost of all benefits paid to employees, which when added to salaries, training, and office costs are the costs of hiring people. Benefits can include medical and life insurance, pensions, and 401(k) savings plans.

employment The number of people in a population who are employed. About 67 percent, or two-thirds, of our non-institutionalized population are working, about 133 million people.

entitlements Social programs in a country, usually directed toward the poor or the elderly. Welfare, unemployment, and Social Security are all considered entitlements in one form or another.

entrepreneur A business person who invests money in manufacturing or service industries, either to create a new company or expand an existing one. Considered the key economic player in a capitalist society. One who sees an opportunity in society and starts a business to fill that need.

equilibrium; equilibrium price The state of balance within an economy where no pressures are forcing changes in supply or demand. Although largely theoretical because of the complexity of an economy, it explains price stability when there is no specific pressure on prices to rise or fall.

equity 1. In investments it refers to common stock, however it is a term that more generally means what you own, such as the equity in your home. It also refers to the net worth of a business, that is total assets minus liabilities equals the business equity. 2. One of two basic methods of raising capital for a company, by common stock, called equity securities. The other method is by bonds, or debt securities.

equity funds A mutual fund that invests in the stock market in one way or another, large cap, small cap, or international equities, for example.

estate The total of what you own, your investments, property, real estate, and any other item of value.

estate planning The strategy through which you provide for others in case something happens to you, and then the eventual distribution of your assets to these people.

estate taxes If someone dies leaving an estate of greater than $600,000 to a non-spouse, under current law, there is a federal estate tax. There may also be a state estate or inheritance tax with or without a $600,000 exemption. Estates left to spouses are not taxed, except in some states.

estimated tax   This is not a problem if you have a regular job and you have the proper amount of taxes deducted from your salary. But if you're self-employed, you have to make quarterly tax payments yourself, estimating what you owe.

Eurodollar Dollars   held by individuals, businesses, and governments outside the United States. Eurodollars are held in Japan, South America, and so forth, so they are not confined to Europe, but since this concept started in Europe, where it remains strong, it retains this name.

eviction   Kicking someone out of a property.

exchange fee   In the world of mutual funds, a fee charged if an investment is shifted from one fund to another within the same company.

exchange rates   The rate of one currency against another. If one American dollar could be exchanged for exactly four French francs, then the exchange rate would be one to four.

ex-dividend   A stock that is traded which will not receive the immediate dividend.

excise tax   A tax on certain consumer items, such as alcohol, tobacco, gas, guns, and airline tickets. These taxes are collected by government departments and used for special purposes, such as highway repair.

executor   The person given the job of settling an estate. The person is specified in the will or is appointed by a court.

exemptions   An exemption is an allowance for each person in the household. For example, being married and having three children results in five exemptions. Each exemption reduces the amount of taxes. The difference between an exemption and a deduction is that a deduction refers to an expense.

exit interview   An interview, sometimes held, with a departing employee to determine why the employee left. These interviews could spot areas the company may want to improve.

extension   An allowed delay, usually of four months, to file your tax return. This is not a delay to pay your taxes, only in filing the forms. You have to pay your taxes, or an estimate of what you owe, by April 15.

fair housing laws Federal, state, and local laws that guarantee people of all races and genders freedom from discrimination when buying, renting, selling, or making any real estate transaction.

fall out of bed Sharp drop in a stock's price, usually in response to negative corporate developments. For example, a stock may fall out of bed if a takeover deal falls apart or if profits in the latest period fall far short of expectations.

family of funds The variety of funds offered by a single mutual fund company.

Fannie Mae (Federal National Mortgage Association or FNMA) The largest secondary mortgage agency in the country. A secondary mortgage agency purchases mortgages from lenders to help with the distribution of funds. Fannie Mae publishes many standard forms for use in residential lending.

Federal Deposit Insurance Corporation (FDIC) The federal governmental insurance organization for banks and depositors. A bank that is FDIC insured will cover deposits (only up to a certain amount) in case the bank fails or runs into financial difficulty.

Federal Home Loan Mortgage Corporation (FHLMC or Freddie Mac) A federal agency that buys mortgages from lenders, giving them more cash to make new mortgages, and gives aid to the FHA and Veteran's Administration-backed loans.

Federal Housing Administration (FHA) The branch of HUD that insures mortgages and offers low-interest guaranteed mortgages to homeowners.

Federal National Mortgage Association (FNMA or Fannie Mae) See Fannie Mae.

Federal Reserve Bank of New York The largest and most active regional Federal Reserve bank.

Federal Reserve Board The governors of the Federal Reserve in Washington plus five presidents of the regional Federal Reserve banks. They meet monthly to decide on such monetary matters as increasing or decreasing the money supply or short-term interest rates.

Federal Reserve Chairman The head of the Federal Reserve (Fed) system, who is the main spokesman for the decisions of the Fed. The chairman testifies in Congress on a regular basis. The chairman usually makes very cautious and general statements to the public so as not to tip off the anticipated actions of the Fed. That could cause investors to buy or sell securities as they speculate about the actions the Fed could take.

Federal Reserve requirements The Federal Reserve (Fed) can change the ratio of reserves a bank is required to hold against deposits. This can tend to increase or decrease activity in the economy. If the Fed increases the reserve requirements, then the bank is restricted in how much money to lend, which tends to slow economic growth. If the Fed decreases the reserve requirements, then more money should expedite economic growth.

Federal Reserve Banking System The system established in our country in 1913 to regulate banking and our money. It is usually referred to simply as the Fed. It consists of twelve District or regional banks, and branch offices in other cities. There is a board of governors, each elected for a term of fourteen years and the Chairman, who is elected for a term of four years.

Federal Reserve (Fed) The common reference to either the Federal Reserve Banking system, board, or chairman that controls the supply of money and regulates banks in the United States.

fee and commission financial planner; fee-based financial planner; fee-only financial planner The three basic compensation methods of financial planners. Fee and commission is charging a set fee for planning and then a commission for buying and selling investments. Fee-based is a more common method where the financial planning charges a percentage of assets of the investor, like a money manager. Fee-only is a small segment of financial planners who simply charge for their time, providing the maximum of objective advice because no investments or insurance are sold.

fee-for-service A term applied to health insurance where you are free to select whichever doctor you wish. This is in contrast to managed care, such as HMOs or PPOs where there is some restriction on which doctors you can see. See health insurance.

FICA (Federal Insurance Contribution Act) The Social Security taxes you and your company pay each year. Currently that rate is 7.65 percent, up to a limit. You and your company both pay it, for a combined total of 15.3 percent. If you're self-employed, you have to pay the full 15.3 percent. Actually, the 7.65 percent is for three different purposes, and three different trust funds. The retirement amount, called the OAS fund (old age and survivors), is 5.6 percent of the total. The disability amount, called the DI (disability), is .6 percent of the total. The medicare amount, called HI (hospital), is 1.45 percent of the total, and is for part A of Medicare. Part B is paid for in part by premiums by older people on Medicare.

filing status Your status generally depends on whether you are single or married, although there are five different filing statuses.

They are: single, married filing jointly, married filing separately, head of household, and qualifying widow(er).

financial commodities; financial futures   Dollars, pounds sterling, francs, Treasury bonds: All of these are commodities, just like sugar and pork bellies. They are traded on specific commodity and futures markets.

financial planner; financial planning   A fairly new financial professional providing a wide range of financial advice, as opposed to just one main area such as investment advice or insurance advice. As a practical matter, financial planning is an ideal that provides advice on all aspects of an individual's finances. In the past an individual would go to a broker for investment advice, an insurance agent for insurance advice, an estate planner for estate planning advice, and so forth. A financial planner is ideally a professional who is able to bring all of these aspects together into a single coherent plan for the individual. See fee and commission financial planner.

financial planning; financial planning seminar   Sometimes offered by companies, a personal session with a planner for executives, or a seminar covering the essential topics of benefits, investments, insurance, and taxes for all employees.

financial statement   A report of a company's balance sheet, income statement, and net worth.

fine tuning   The delicate process of keeping the economy on a steady growth pattern, without too much growth and without a recession. Through mainly monetary policy, the Federal Reserve tries to calibrate economic growth with the various financial tools it controls, such as adjusting the interest rates and reserve requirements. See federal funds rate, discount rate, and the Federal Reserve requirements.

first mortgage   The mortgage that takes precedence over any other mortgages or liens against a property, such as a second mortgage.

fiscal policy   Policies and actions taken by the federal government to stimulate the economy by increasing (or decreasing) government spending or increasing (or decreasing) taxes. The President and Congress involve themselves in these policies, which are in contrast to monetary policies and practices. Monetary policies have to do with increasing or decreasing the available money in the economy, which is generally controlled by the Federal Reserve.

fiscal year   Any twelve-month period that may or may not coincide with a calendar year. A fiscal year is usually selected to include a complete season for a company. For instance, a ski resort would probably have a fiscal year from July 1 through June 30.

fixed exchange rates   Currency exchange rates that are fixed, as opposed to floating, as they are today. Fixed rates existed among the developed nations from 1944 to 1973. See Bretton Woods agreement.

fixed-income securities   A more technical name for bonds, notes and preferred stock. They are investments that pay a fixed amount of interest, hence their name.

flexible spending accounts   A company plan that allows pre-tax money to pay for eligible unreimbursed medical (such as eyeglasses and dental care) and dependent day-care expenses.

flex-time   Work schedules that allow employees to choose their starting and quitting times, usually within certain limits. Employees may be able to choose either end of the designated core time. Thus, an employee may be required to work the core hours, say, from 10 A.M. to 3 P.M. and might then be allowed to select the additional three hours before or after, or both, around the core times.

float   The initial public offering of a security; if investors go for it, the stock issue or bond floats.

floating exchange rates   Currency exchange rates that are not fixed, but move on a weekly and daily basis. See Bretton Woods agreement.

floating mortgage rate   A variable mortgage rate that moves according to some other rate, such as the treasury bill rate.

floor (the floor of an exchange)   The actual trading area at an exchange, such as the New York Stock Exchange (NYSE).

foreign exchange   Changing money from one country's currency to another. The foreign exchange market is not one physical place; it is a network of computers, and of course that corner bank in Paris, or wherever you happen to be traveling.

401(k)   plan A popular retirement-type plan offered by companies. See defined-contribution plan.

fraud   Intentionally deceiving others and thereby causing harm, usually financial harm rather than physical harm.

Freddie Mac   The nickname for the Federal Home Loan Mortgage Corporation, which buys and packages mortgages, encouraging lenders to offer more mortgages to individuals.

free and clear   Describes a property with no mortgages or liens outstanding.

free trade   The minimum restrictions on the free flow of goods and services between countries

fringe benefits   Company benefits such as vacation, holidays, and pensions. During World War II these benefits were thought to be "on the fringe of wages." Since these benefits are now common the term is clearly out-of-date.

front money   The money needed to get a project going; the money an investor needs before the financing is in place.

full employment   The percentage of people in an economy who are working, out of those who can work, or who want to. This figure is generally held to be about 95 percent, not 100 percent, because some people can't find work they want or some people are simply between jobs temporarily.

full-service broker   A broker who will not only buy and sell stocks and other securities, but will provide advice to customers. A full-service broker charges a higher commission than a discount broker or deep-discount broker, but these two do not offer investment advice.

fund managers   Since a mutual fund is a collection of many individual stocks or bonds, it must be managed. The professional investment company that does this job is called the fund manager.

fundamental analysis   One of two approaches to analyzing the stock market. Fundamental analysis relies primarily on economic supply and demand, business earnings, balance sheets, and economic factors of a particular company or its business sector to determine if a stock, or group of stocks, should be bought or sold. This is opposed to technical analysis which relies primarily on market volume or price movements to determine the best time to buy or sell stocks. See technical analysis.

futures; futures contracts   Obligations to buy or sell a commodity at a specific day at a specific price. Futures contracts always expire on the third Friday of each month. Because the investor is investing in an actual commodity, it generally is considered the riskiest of all investments. They can have big payoffs, but most individual investors in futures regret having ever been bit by the futures bug.

futures exchanges; futures trading   Futures contracts are traded on special futures exchanges.

Galbraith, John Kenneth (1908–   )   An American economist and writer who is associated with strong government intervention in the economy. His 1958 book *The Affluent Society* gave a name to the remarkable economic growth after World War II.

garnish To take money out of someone's salary in order to pay a court settlement. The person who takes the money out (usually the employer) is the garnishee; the court order to have the money taken out is called a garnishment.

GDP (Gross Domestic Product) See gross domestic product.

general obligation bond (GO) Generally a state-issued bond backed by the "full faith and credit" of that state. This is in contrast to revenue bonds, such as a bridge, tunnel, or highway authority. These revenue bonds are backed only by the revenue from that bridge, tunnel, or toll highway. General obligation bonds are less risky than revenue bonds because of the broader and more secure nature of the financial backing, and usually pay a slightly lower interest rate.

gift tax A tax required on a monetary gift, or gifts, but only after a specified annual amount. That amount is generally $10,000 per person per year. A few states also impose a gift tax.

Ginnie Mae (Government National Mortgage Association or GNMA) A federal corporation under HUD that purchases FHA-insured mortgages on the secondary market and issues mortgage-backed securities that are federally insured.

global fund A type of mutual fund that invests in securities in any country including the United States. This is in contrast to an international fund which invests in only countries outside the United States.

global market The ties among all the markets of the world—when trading stops in one, it begins in another, and the events in one country affect trading in another. The number of international companies as well as electronic worldwide trading also contribute to this global market.

GNP (Gross National Product) See gross national product.

Gold A metal that is held in high regard around the world. At one time it was a standard to which currencies had to be converted so international trade could be equated between countries.

gold standard At one time the value of currency was based on the value of metals such as gold and silver. This was called the gold standard. The gold standard disappeared in 1971, when the United States stopped backing its currency with gold.

good 'til cancelled (GTC) An order with your broker that stands until it either is executed or you cancel it. Often, however, you may want to make a stop order or a limit order (these will limit at what price or how much the broker will buy or sell). You should tell the broker whether to make your limitations GTC or a day order.

greenback Slang for dollar.

gross domestic product (GDP) The measurement of how an economy is doing. It measures the total output of goods and services within a country measured at market prices, on a quarterly and annual basis. It does not count intermediate goods, only goods used for final consumption, because it is assumed that the value of intermediate goods is built into the prices of the final goods. The U.S. used to rely on the GNP, which measured the output by American citizens and businesses no matter where they were, here or overseas. Starting in December 1991, the Commerce Department officially changed to reporting GDP, mainly because that is how the other major countries measure and report their economic output. The GDP measurement is only slightly lower for the United States than was the GNP (less than one-third of one percent). Some production by U.S. companies is lost since only production within a country is considered, but there are also gains: The Honda production plant in California is reported in our GDP, for example.

gross income 1. The total income from a business or property. 2. To the IRS, gross income is gross taxable income: salary, any investment earnings, and any other income subject to income tax.

gross margin; gross profit; gross profit margin Sales minus the cost of goods sold, or the amount of revenues before administrative expenses and taxes are applied.

gross national product (GNP) The previous standard for measuring the goods and services produced each year. It measured the total production by American citizens and businesses not only here but around the world. It has been replaced with GDP, because the new measurement is consistent with how other countries measure their economies. See gross domestic product.

gross revenues; gross sales The total sales amount, without any adjustments for discounts or returns.

group policy A company benefit where because of sheer numbers, a company can get a better medical or life insurance rate than you could on your own. Thus, a group rate is an attractive rate.

growth An increase in business activity. This is the main subject of economics. How and why business activities increase or decrease has been the subject of a number of theories by economists and actions by governments.

growth and income fund; growth fund Mutual funds that invest primarily in growth stocks. Growth and income funds will stress income more, through higher paying income stocks, whereas growth funds stress growth only. However, during most periods the total return of both will be similar.

growth stocks Individual stocks that are primarily geared to growth with little or no emphasis on income through dividends. Some growth stocks will pay no dividends.

growth versus value A technical and potentially important distinction between common stocks or equity mutual funds. A growth stock or fund has a higher than average P/E (price/earnings) ratio whereas a value stock or fund has a lower than average P/E ratio. Although there are other measures used, the P/E ratio is the most commonly used. One is based on the theory that if stock has a higher P/E ratio then the market has identified and recognized that company as a good investment. The other theory is that a value stock, lower P/E ratio, will have a greater potential to increase and therefore is a better investment. Thus the two theories and two approaches.

guaranteed invest contracts (GICs) A common investment option in your 401(k) that pays a relatively attractive rate of interest, because a high number of employees were expected to select that option.

guaranteed loan A loan by a country or international agency to stimulate growth in a targeted country.

guaranteed mortgage A mortgage that has some second party backing up the borrower in case he or she cannot pay.

hard currency Gold and silver coins, also known as specie. In the old days, people preferred hard currency to flimsy paper currency.

hardship withdrawals A provision in a 401(k) that allows a special distribution for a difficult personal situation, because of which an employee is strapped for money.

health insurance A general term for a variety of medical coverages at a company, such as comprehensive or major medical, and through such means as fee-for-service, managed care, HMO, or PPO. Often a monthly premium is necessary. When medical services are needed, there is often a deductible and/or a co-payment.

hedge; hedging; hedgers Investors who protect themselves against an existing investment position by buying or selling other offsetting securities, such as options, to protect their original investments.

hedge fund   A high risk fund that allows the investment manager free reign. No conservative investing style here, with selling short, options, borrowing money, and any particular strategy that offers very high returns, with of course very high risks.

HH bonds   U.S. savings bonds that pay interest semi-annually just like a regular bond. Currently you can only obtain HH bonds by the redemption from EE bonds, which is a tax-free exchange. HH bonds are in contrast to EE bonds that accumulate interest until cashed in.

hidden assets   Assets of a company that are undervalued or ignored.

high-wage strategy   An economic policy by a country to emphasize and encourage high wages for its workers, either by wages alone or a combination of wages and benefits.

high-yield bonds; high-yield fund   Bonds, or mutual funds that invest in bonds, that pay a higher rate of return than normal, because they are rated lower than average. They are also called junk bonds because they are so lowly rated. They are rated below triple-B. Although they are the riskiest of bonds, they potentially provide investors high income.

historical costs   An accounting method using the original cost of an item, in contrast to inflation accounting, in which the effects of inflation on an item are shown.

HMO (health maintenance organization)   See health insurance.

holding period return   A quick calculation, and not a very meaningful one, that determines how much an investor has made on an investment over the time it was held. The profit plus any interest or dividends is divided by the original price.

home banking   Service offered by banks allowing consumers and small businesses to perform many banking functions at home through computers, telephones, and cable television links to the bank, thereby providing them with a number of convenience services. Bank customers are able to shift money between accounts, apply for loans and make loan payments, pay bills, check balances, and buy and sell securities, among other services. As home banking becomes easier and more convenient to use, more and more consumers sign up for it. It offers the advantage of privacy, speed, accuracy and the ability to perform transactions at any time. Most banks charge an extra fee for access to home banking services. Home banking does not currently offer the ability to obtain cash, for which customers must still visit a bank teller or automatic teller machine.

home run Large gain by an investor in a short period of time. Someone who aims to hit an investment home run may be looking for a potential takeover target, for example, since takeover bids result in sudden price spurts. Such investing is inherently more risky than the strategy of holding for the long run.

housing starts A figure representing the number of new homes started in the construction field. The housing starts figure is a leading economic indicator.

human capital Workers, seen as an asset in the economy. Increasing employee training or education increases human capital.

hybrid pension plans Pension plans that have features of both defined contribution and defined benefit plans. Two such plans are called money purchase and target benefit plans.

hyperinflation Very rapid increase in inflation. Sometimes called galloping inflation. We may find it hard to imagine in the United States, but some countries have experienced inflation rates as high as 50 percent to 100 percent per year. After World War I in Europe, a number of countries experienced very high inflation.

hypothecate To pledge securities for a margin account as a form of collateral without giving up ownership of the securities.

immunization An investing technique by institutional firms to protect their portfolio against interest rate fluctuations.

in the money See at the money.

income Money received; income may be a combination of earnings and investment income.

income dividends; income distributions One of the ways a mutual fund pays its equity investors. Dividends earned by stocks are accumulated and paid to investors during the year according to a schedule.

income statement A key financial statement showing the company's revenues (sales), expenses, and net income (profits) during a period of time, at least annually and often each quarter. Whereas a balance sheet shows the condition of a company at a particular point in time, the income statement shows the results of the company's operations during a specific time frame, such as from January 1st through December 31st. It is also called the profit and loss statement. As an example of an income statement:

income stocks Stocks that pay regular dividends.

income tax A tax imposed on personal or business income.

index fund   A mutual fund that matches an index, such as the S&P 500 index, to provide a return that duplicates the overall market. Because mutual fund managers have a hard time beating the market averages, index funds have become very popular. Index funds also match other market averages, such as small cap stocks and international stocks.

index options   A right to buy or sell at a set price on a set day an option on an index, such as the S&P 500. It is a bet that a certain market index will rise or fall at a certain time.

indexes   The most famous index is the Dow Jones Industrial Index, thirty major stocks that are considered a bellwether to the overall market. The most used index by professionals is the S&P 500 index, which is the 500 largest capitalized stocks in the country. It is considered more useful to professionals because it is broader based and is considered a better representation of the overall economy.

indirect costs; indirect labor; indirect materials   Costs that are difficult to identify and charge to a product, and thus are lumped together as factory overhead and charged generally.

individual retirement account (IRA)   The contribution of up to $2,000 per year of salary into a special account with a bank, mutual fund, or brokerage account, for your retirement. If you are covered at work with a pension or 401(k)-type plan and you are earning too much, your contribution will not be tax deductible, although you may still make the contribution.

inefficient markets   Markets that are not widely analyzed. Inefficient markets may be interesting speculative investments for those who are willing to take risks that are difficult to quantify.

inflation   A rise in prices, that could potentially effect investments. Higher inflation could mean less attractive bond prices and less attractive stock prices. Short term higher inflation generally is bad news to the markets.

inheritance tax   A state tax imposed on an estate by calculating the tax according to who receives the money. For instance, if a spouse or child receives it there is generally less tax imposed. If a distant relative receives it, then a higher tax is imposed. This is in contrast to an estate tax, which is simply based on the total estate, regardless of who receives it. Not all states have an inheritance or estate tax.

initial margin requirement   The deposit an investor puts down on a securities transaction, borrowing the rest from the brokerage firm. The Federal Reserve determines the minimum margin as a way to curb over speculation in the market.

initial public offering (IPO) When a company first goes public, offering stock for public purchase, it's called appropriately an IPO. Some IPOs cause a stir because many investors believe its a time to make a killing, whereas experience has shown that IPOs often drop in price after an initial flurry of interest and reality sets in.

insider A term used with respect to executives who have limitations on when they may exercise stock options because they have inside information about the company.

insider trading Since executives of a company have specific information about the company and company actions that could affect its stock price, they are restricted in trading in their stock. Trading based on that inside information may be illegal. The Securities and Exchange Commission (SEC) monitors insider trading closely to preserve the integrity of the market. See technical analysis.

institutional investors Firms or organizations that invest large sums of money in investments. Insurance companies and pension systems are examples of institutional investors.

insurance The business of offering financial protection due to specific losses, such as life or property insurance.

insured A person or company who is covered for specific risks by auto insurance or health insurance.

insured bonds Municipal bonds, primarily state revenue bonds, that have purchased insurance against non-payment of interest or principal. The insurance results in a less risky bond, and a lower interest rate necessary to be paid by the state.

insurer The insurance company that sells policies and insures against a variety of risks.

interest 1. Money paid on bonds, notes, and money market instruments. 2. Charge for the use of money during a period of time.

interest cost The expense of using borrowed money.

interest-only loan A special loan in which the borrower pays back the interest for a set time and then the principal in one lump sum at the end of the loan period.

interest rate curve See yield curve.

interest rates Rates of payments from bonds, notes, money market funds, CDs, or savings accounts. The rate of return on an interest-bearing account.

intermediate bonds Bonds or notes that have a maturity generally of from two to ten years. They are considered less risky than long-term bonds, which have maturities of twenty to thirty years.

internal audit; internal auditor An employee of a company, usually in an independent department, who is responsible for auditing various aspects of the accounting procedures, checking for fraud, and promoting efficient operations.

internal controls Methods and policies to minimize errors and fraud and promote efficient operations.

internal rate of return (IRR) The rate of interest that discounts a stream of payments to a present value, providing the effective annual return on investment over the life of a project.

Internal Revenue Service (IRS) A branch of the United States Treasury Department that collects income tax and enforces the tax code. It can impose penalties, seize property, or take whatever it feels is necessary to collect taxes.

international fund A type of mutual fund that invests in securities in any country but not the United States. This is in contrast to a global fund which invests in any country including the United States.

International Monetary Fund (IMF) Created at the Bretton Woods agreement in 1944, it encouraged international cooperation in monetary matters, including the fixing of exchange rates within a narrow range. It also provides economic advice to less developed countries. In 1967, it created Special Drawing Rights (SDR), which was intended to be an international currency but which has been of very limited value. In 1990, the IMF had 152 member countries, while in 1996, there were 181 members. See Bretton Woods.

International Trade Commission (ITC) A United States agency organized in 1974 to investigate and make recommendations about damage to our domestic industry by foreign businesses. Dumping is one of the practices the Commission considers seriously. See dumping.

International Trade Organization (ITO) An international body proposed in 1947 with the UN Organization, but never fully ratified. GATT now performs the functions envisioned for the ITO.

intestate Dying without a will. The state laws then determine who gets what; usually everything goes to spouses and children.

intrapreneur An employee whose company gives her more flexibility and financial support to create new products or services, with the intention of duplicating the small company spirit within a large company.

inventory The amount of materials stored for use in production.

investment The economic use of capital to increase the production of goods and services.

investment banker A firm that underwrites or sells new securities to the general public.

investment clubs Small groups of investors pooling their money and commonly deciding on what investments to make. Well run investment clubs have provided better than average investment returns.

investment grade Bonds with a top rating, of AAA, AA, A, or BBB by Moody's or Standard & Poor's.

investment income Income received from various investments and taxed as unearned income.

Investor's Daily A daily newspaper for active investors.

invoice A document sent to a purchaser showing the sale, delivery date, and the amount due the company.

IRA See Individual Retirement Account.

joint and survivor options Pension plan options an employee selects before retiring. An employee may make the option of taking less money upon retirement, but providing for a survivor payment when the employee dies. See pension plan.

joint return If you are married, you and your spouse will generally file a joint return. If separated, you may elect to file separate returns so you are not responsible for the other person's taxes.

junk bonds See high-yield bonds.

Keogh plan Pronounced KEY-oh, it's a pension plan for the self-employed and partnerships. Keogh plans can take different forms, such as a defined benefit plan, a defined contribution plan, or a hybrid plan. These plans are often called H.R. 10 plans.

kiddie tax The tax for a minor under the age of fourteen on investment income over a certain amount.

kiting Various illegal practices of creating false bank account balances by altering the account books, issuing checks in excess of existing balances, or altering the checks themselves.

Krugerrand A South African gold coin.

labor In economic terms, a factor of production. It includes not only the physical number of employees, but their skills and experience.

labor demand As one of the factors of production, it is a force that can cause prices to increase or decrease. As the demand for labor increases in a growth economy, wages, salaries, and benefits tend to rise.

labor-intensive Industries that require more labor than average to either start or sustain a company, such as the automotive industry. This is in contrast to capital-intensive industries, such as oil refineries or chemical plants.

labor market The economic market where wages, salaries and the conditions of employment are determined by market forces.

labor force By the U.S. Bureau of Labor Statistics definition, the labor force consists of people over the age of sixteen who are employed.

lagging indicators Data, ratios, or other figures that tend to come later in an economic cycle, such as a build-up of inventories and rising prices.

laid off Fired; may also be used for the positions that have been eliminated—"lay offs."

laissez-faire An economic theory stating that business would be better off without government interference. In economic lingo, it is allowing free markets with a minimum of government interference so as to best allocate a nation's resources.

large-cap fund; large-cap stocks The term "cap" stands for "capitalization," meaning a large company with more than average shares and often with more than average earnings. Picking the right large-cap stocks can mean good investment returns. See small-cap fund/stocks.

lead charitable trust A trust to provide income for a specific charity while the person who sets it up is alive, but when the person dies, the money goes generally to a family member. It allows an ongoing donation to a charity through interest on the trust, while the principal is retained for the family.

lease A contract to use equipment, computers, or buildings instead of owning them outright.

legal tender Money that, by law of the government, must be accepted as a payment. On the United States dollar, and other denominations, you will see the words "This note is legal tender for all debts, public and private."

Lehman Brothers bond index A bond index that measures the total return of a diversified portfolio of corporate bonds.

letter of credit A bank promise to pay once certain conditions are met, usually the shipment of goods.

leverage; leveraged The use of assets, capital, or funds to create a greater return than normal, often by borrowing additional funds.

The additional funds are then invested in a higher-risk investment, with hopes of greater-than-normal returns.

leveraged buyout (LBO) Using a small percentage of the total money involved to takeover a company. Investors typically make LBOs by borrowing against the assets of the company they are taking over and repaying the loan, from company profits after the takeover is complete.

liability A legal term that refers to the extent to which a person or company is legally bound to make good on a loss or damage resulting from their actions.

liability insurance Protection against any claims made if someone is injured or property is damaged on your premises.

liable To be held responsible for something.

lien A legal interest in a property to secure a payment of debt.

life insurance An arrangement with a life insurance company to pay a benefit, usually a lump-sum payment, to the surviving spouse or family if an employee dies.

limit order Instructing a stock broker to buy only when the stock falls to a specific price or selling when the stock rises to a specific price. The order may be good until canceled (GTC) or a day order.

limited partnership An investment in which the investor "participates" in that profits and losses are passed through directly to the investor. The general partner runs the partnership whereas the investor's liability is "limited" and does not participate in the management of the partnership. At one time limited partnerships were popular as tax write-offs when tax rates were quite high, now they are primarily for providing income. These investments are very illiquid and cannot be bought and sold freely. Typically a partnership purchases property (real estate), or items (equipment leasing), or mineral rights (oil and gas) for a specific period of time, usually 5 to 7 years, and then sells the property and hopefully returns a gain to the investors. These investments have fallen out of favor because of their poor performance.

liquid Any asset that can be immediately converted into cash. A checking account is a liquid asset because it can be used in the same basic way as cash. The process of converting assets into cash is called liquidating.

liquidate The act of selling assets, usually to pay debts.

liquidation The process of closing down a company, including selling the assets of the company and paying creditors.

litigation   To engage in a legal process.

load funds   In mutual funds, the commission charged to the buyer of the fund. A front-end load fund is one in which the commission is paid up front when the fund is purchased. A back-end load fund is one in which the commission is paid when the fund is sold. A no-load means that there's no commission on the purchase of the fund. A low load fund has a low commission.

loans   The borrowing of money by individuals, businesses, or governments to finance activities.

local taxes   Taxes collected through local municipalities, in addition to state and federal taxes. These can be for local schools and libraries.

long bond   A bond with a maturity of usually longer that ten years. The popular thirty-year Treasury bond is often quoted as the "long" rate. An investor who buys these bonds is said to be "going long."

long-term debt   Notes or bonds issued by a company, usually longer than one year, or longer than current liabilities.

loose money   See easy money.

lump-sum distribution   The distribution of all pension money or 401(k) money in a single sum. Because these types of plans are considered qualified, which means they meet certain criteria, they then qualify for special tax considerations. These tax advantages include being able to put the money into a Rollover IRA and in some cases have special averaging tax treatment applied to them.

luxury tax   An excise tax on specific expensive items. Luxury cars, very expensive jewelry, and large boats are examples of items that may incur a luxury tax. Most of these taxes end up reaping little revenue, because some wealthy taxpayers avoid buying those items. The luxury boat tax caused such high unemployment within the U.S. boat industry that it was repealed.

M1, M2, M3   A measurement of how much "money" there is in an economy. M1 is currency and checking accounts, M2 is savings accounts, and M3 is money market funds. These are often called monetary aggregates because M2 contains M1, and M3 contains M1 and M2.

Ma Bell   Nickname for AT&T Corporation. Before the Bell System was broken up in 1984, AT&T controlled both local and long distance telephone service in the United States. After the breakup, local phone service was performed by the seven regional phone companies and AT&T concentrated on long distance, telecommunications research, equipment and computer manufacturing. Even though it no longer enjoys the monopoly it once had, people still refer to AT&T as Ma Bell. The stock is also a component of the Dow Jones Industrial Average, and is one of the most widely held and actively traded stocks on the New York Stock Exchange.

macroeconomics Type of economics dealing with aggregate aspects of the economy, such as supply and demand, how markets work, and the interrelations between countries and economies. Some of the subjects it covers are inflation, unemployment, fiscal and monetary policies, and the balance of payments. It is the study of the big picture, the whole economy, in contrast to microeconomics, which studies how individual people or companies operate within the economy.

major medical Health insurance primarily for large surgical, hospital, and other medical expenses.

managed care A term applied to health insurance, specifically HMOs and PPOs where there is some sort of restriction on which doctors you can see. This is in contrast to fee-for-service where you are free to select whichever doctor you wish. See health insurance.

mandatory minimum withdrawal-age seventy For IRAs (individual retirement accounts) withdrawals must begin at age seventy. These mandatory withdrawals are somewhat modest, often only about 5 percent, but if not, then there is a penalty of 50 percent of what should have been taken out. This rule was intended to make sure income taxes are paid by everyone, because withdrawals are taxed at ordinary tax rates.

margin The difference between cost and selling price. See gross margin.

margin; margin account; margin call A line of credit with a broker. If you have a margin account, you can leverage, or borrow, up to a certain percent of the price of a stock from your broker. If the value of a stock that has been bought on margin falls to a certain level, your broker will make a margin call: either you put more money into the margin account or sell the stock and take the loss. It's the broker's way of minimizing the risk in your investment.

marginal cost The cost of producing "one more." The more quantity produced, usually the lower the cost of each item. Because a company wants to make a profit, it is important to produce a quantity high enough to make a satisfactory profit.

market An economy in which business transactions take place.

market breadth The proportion of stocks rising in an upward market or falling in a declining market. See technical analysis.

market correction   See correction.

market cycles   Up and down shifts in the market as economic and business activities shift. The market goes up in a bull market and inevitably backs down in a bear market.

market economy   An economy in which the free market operates.

market forces   The dynamics of supply and demand and of price movements.

market jitters   State of widespread fear among investors, which may cause them to sell stocks and bonds, pushing prices downward. Investors may fear lower corporate earnings, negative economic news, tightening of credit by the Federal Reserve, foreign currency fluctuations, or many other factors. In some cases, news may be good, but is interpreted as bad because investors are so fearful. For example, investors may think that positive economic or corporate earnings news is putting more pressure on the Federal Reserve to raise interest rates, which would hurt stock and bond prices.

market momentum   The rate of change of stock prices in the market by volume. See technical analysis.

market order   An order for a broker to immediately buy or sell. You are thus willing to accept what the market offers.

market timing   An ideal investing strategy of switching into stocks before they rise and switching out of them before they decline. Since investors cannot predict when the market will rise or fall, it is a strategy investors grasp for, but are frustrated in executing.

market value   1. Generally, the price at which a product or asset can be sold. Also called fair market value. 2. The most probable price a property will sell for in a competitive market with an informed buyer and seller who are not under any duress during the sale.

marriage penalty   A facet, generally of past tax legislation, by which many married couples paid more together than they would have as two single people. This problem was minimized in 1981, though some high-income married couples are still penalized.

May Day   May 1, 1975, a monumental day on Wall Street when fixed commissions were eliminated, ushering in considerable competition for investors' business. See Big Bang.

meeting the margin   If the value of your stock investments drop and your broker makes a margin call (asks you to put more money in the account), you either meet the margin by putting in that extra money to keep your investment, or you must sell your stock.

microeconomics The study of how individuals or companies behave in the economy, versus the entire economy as a whole, which is the study of macroeconomics. See macroeconomics.

middle class A general term applied by economists and politicians. It is the class of people above the poverty line and below the wealthy population. It is said to consist of people earning from about $20,000 to $75,000 a year.

minimum wage The lowest wage that can be legally paid by a business.

mint A place where our government manufactures money. The process of making coins is called minting. In the United States, coins are minted at one of the three government mints: Denver, Philadelphia, or San Francisco.

miscellaneous deductions A category of itemized deductions that must exceed 2 percent of your adjusted gross income. If the total of this category exceeds this percent, then the amount over can be deducted.

mixed economy An economy that has features of capitalism (free markets) and socialism (government control).

Modern Portfolio Theory (MPT) The prevailing overall theory of investing, consisting of several key tenets. Namely, that investors are more concerned with risk than return (that is, investors are risk adverse), that capital markets are efficient (that is, almost all information that can be known is known), and that asset allocation is the most important strategy (versus, individual stock or mutual fund selection).

momentum See market momentum.

Mommy track When a woman has a child, there may be an attitude within a company that she is not serious about her career. Such an attitude can lead to missed opportunities for the woman, who may indeed be very serious about her career. A woman on a "mommy track" will get pay increases but not the opportunities for advancement that other employees get.

monetarism The economic school of thought that believes that changes in the supply of money are the main determinant in the economy. Too much money leads to increases in prices (inflation), resulting in an economic boom. Booms, however, always lead to recessions. Too little money levels or decreases prices, and potentially causes an economic recession. Since the Federal Reserve (Fed) controls the money supply, the Fed should gauge the optimum money supply to continually sustain growth without much inflation.

monetary policy   Policies and actions taken usually by the Federal Reserve to increase or decrease the amount of money available in the economy. This is meant to either stimulate or slow down the economy. These policies are in contrast to fiscal policy, which are actions by the President and Congress to increase (decrease) spending and taxes.

money   There are many definitions for money, but it is mainly thought of as the commodity that a country officially designates for people to use to purchase goods and services.

Money magazine   A popular magazine for individual investors.

money market; money market instruments   Short-term investments, either money market mutual funds or individual short-term investments such as Treasury bills, commercial paper, or bankers' acceptances.

money market account   Market-sensitive bank account that has been offered since December 1982. Under Depository Institutions Deregulatory Committee rules, such accounts had a minimum of $1000 (eliminated in 1986) and three checks may be drawn per month, although unlimited transfers may be carried out at an automated teller machine. The funds are therefore liquid—that is, they are available to depositors at any time without penalty. The interest rate is generally comparable to rates on money market mutual funds, though any individual bank's rate may be higher or lower. These accounts are insured by the Federal Deposit Insurance Corporation

money market fund   Open-ended mutual fund that invests in commercial paper, banker's acceptances, repurchase agreements, government securities, certificates of deposit, and other highly liquid and safe securities, and pays money market rates of interest. Launched in the middle 1970s, these funds were especially popular in the early 1980s when interest rates and inflation soared. Management's fee is less than 1% of an investor's assets; interest over and above that amount is credited to shareholders monthly. The fund's net asset value remains a constant $1 a share—only the interest rate goes up or down. Such funds usually offer the convenience of check writing privileges.

Most funds are not federally insured, but some are covered by private insurance. Some funds invest only in government-backed securities, which give shareholders an extra degree of safety.

Many money market funds are part of fund families. This means that investors can switch their money from one fund to another and back again without charge. Money in an asset management account usually is automatically swept into a money market fund until the accountholder decides where to invest it next.

money purchase plan See hybrid pension plan.

money supply The amount of money a population has to spend at any given time. The money supply includes cash and checking accounts, but it also includes assets that can be sold and turned into cash. The money supply is measured by the monetary aggregates M1, M2, and M3.

monopoly Any market in which one company or individual controls the market and, as a result, can set the price of a good.

Morningstar mutual fund service A popular mutual fund reporting service for individual investors.

mortgage A legal document for a loan in which property is held as collateral for the loan on the property. It is the promissory note that actually designates the loan payment schedule.

mortgage banker/broker A person who will match a buyer to a mortgage lender, usually for a fee as some percentage of the desired loan amount.

mortgage term The amount of time within which the mortgage loan must be paid back.

mortgagee/mortgagor In legal talk, the one who has a mortgage (you)/the one who is giving the mortgage (the bank).

most favored nation (MFN) The trade conditions given to a country equal to the best conditions given to anyone else. This term sounds better than it pretends. Most countries have most favored nation status with the United States. It's just an agreement that gives those countries the assurances that if any better trading conditions are given to one particular country, it will automatically be given to all who have that status.

moving averages A rolling average of the stock market performance for a specified number of days, frequently around 200 days. That is, each day one more day is added, and one subtracted, so the last 200 days is averaged. It is helpful in showing a general trend in the market. See technical analysis.

multilateral trade An agreement between many countries on international trade issues. This is in contrast to bilateralism, which is an agreement between just two countries. See GATT.

multiple listing service (MLS) A computerized service of real estate sales listings, distributed among different real estate agents so that more than one office will work on the sale of the same property.

municipal bonds (munis) Bonds issued by municipalities—cities, towns, states, counties—usually for public improvement or operating budgets.

mutual fund A collection of investments managed by a professional investment firm. Mutual funds have become very popular versus buying individual stocks or bonds. Instead of trying to select the right stocks, the investor tries to select the right mutual fund. The three main types of mutual funds are stock, bond, and money market funds.

mutual fund fees The variety of fees charge by mutual funds, such as exchange fees, management fees, redemption fees and 12b-1 fees.

NAFTA (North American Free-Trade Agreement) A three-country trade agreement between Canada, Mexico, and the United States concluded in 1993. It has been a controversial agreement, particularly in the United States, where critics charge that jobs will be lost to lower-wage workers in Mexico. This agreement follows the 1988 agreement between Canada and the United States in a similar free-trade agreement.

naked option A naked option is the opposite of a covered option: In this very risky venture, you are selling an option that will give someone else the ability to buy something you don't yet own. You may have to buy shares of a commodity at the agreed upon price to fill the contract.

nanny tax A tax that has been controversial and complicated to determine. The compensation of people hired to care for children is considered salary, so certain taxes must be paid, including FICA or Social Security taxes.

NASD (National Association of Security Dealers) A group of brokers linked by an electronic network called the over-the-counter (OTC) market. It was established in 1939 to regulate the OTC market.

NASDAQ; NASDAQ issues; NASDAQ system The National Association of Security Dealers (NASDAQ) automated system for over-the-counter issues of almost 5,000 companies' stock prices. A daily listing of the largest and most actively traded stocks on the NASDAQ.

National Association of Realtors (NAR) The main trade and professional organization for the real estate industry; includes such professional organizations as the American Institute of Real Estate Appraisers (AIREA), American Society of Real Estate Counselors, Institute of Real Estate Management, and Realtors National Marketing Institute, among many others.

national debt Owed by the federal government. The national debt is made up of such debt obligations as Treasury bills, Treasury notes, and Treasury bonds. Congress imposes a ceiling on the national debt, which has been increased on occasion when accumulated deficits near the ceiling. In the mid-1990s, the national debt stood at more than $5 trillion. The interest due on the national debt is one of the major expenses of the federal government. The national debt, which is the total debt accumulated by the government over many decades, should not be confused with the federal budget deficit, which is the excess of spending over income by the federal government in one fiscal year.

National Register of Historic Places A listing of historic sites that are considered worthy of preservation. Homes and buildings that are registered must be maintained according to strict guidelines.

negative cash flow What you get when you spend more money than you receive during any period.

net asset value (NAV) A daily mutual fund value calculation that equals the value of the stocks or bonds in the fund divided by the total number of shares. Thus it's an average price per mutual fund share.

net earnings The money made after deducting all expenses and taxes from gross earnings.

net income ratio The ratio of the net operating income to the effective gross income multiplier.

net operating income Income made by a company after deducting operating expenses but before deducting income taxes and mortgage debt.

net worth All a company's or individual's assets minus its liabilities.

New York Stock Exchange (NYSE) The first, and foremost, stock exchange in the country, founded in 1792. It's considered to be the center of our stock market action. Results of trades conducted on the NYSE are published every business day.

Nobel Prize for economics The Nobel Prizes are awards given to those the Nobel committee deems to have made significant achievements in the fields of science. It was founded by a bequest by Alfred Nobel, the inventor of dynamite. The first prize was awarded in 1901, but it was not until 1969 that a prize was designated for economics.

no-brainer Term used to describe a market the direction of which has become obvious, and therefore requires little or no analysis.

This means that most of the stocks will go up in a strong bull market and fall in a bear market, so that it does not matter very much which stock investors buy or sell.

no-fault insurance   Auto insurance payments regardless of who was at fault.

nominal GDP   The total domestic output in current dollars, or what they are worth today. This is in contrast to real GDP, which measures domestic output according to what they would have been earlier, given what prices were then. See gross domestic product.

NOW account (Negotiable order of withdrawal)   A bank checking/ savings account earning slightly higher interest. There is usually restrictions on how many checks can be written and minimum balances required. Super NOW accounts earn even slightly more.

no-load; no-load fund   Mutual funds that charge no commissions, or brokerage fees.

odd lot   An order to purchase common stock shares that is not a multiple of 100. Brokers charge extra for odd lot purchases and sales.

offering price   The price of a stock or mutual fund is offered to the public.

offset   When a trade is neutralized by an opposite transaction. For example, a contract to buy a commodity can be offset by a contract to sell a commodity.

offshore banking   Banking operations that are in small non-regulated, or low-regulated, countries, mainly islands. These are places where the small economies are geared to be business friendly to encourage such banking.

OPEC (Organization of Petroleum Exporting Countries)   A group of mainly Arabic countries that produce oil. OPEC has engaged in sometimes dramatic increases in the price of oil, especially in the 1970s. One of the most effective cartels in recent history.

open interest   The number of futures contracts that have not been offset.

open outcry   You've probably seen those movies where traders are all standing around yelling. Orders on the futures exchanges are called out publicly in a cool system where he or she who yells loudest will probably do best.

open-end fund   A fund that has unlimited shares it can sell. The more the public wants to buy, the more it sells. The majority of mutual funds are open-end funds.

operating budget   The financial plan, or budget, for revenue and expenses of a company.

operating expenses   Expenses a company incurs to keep production of goods and services going.

options   The right to buy or sell a commodity for a set price up until a specific end date. An option to buy a security is called a call option. An option to sell a security is called a put option.

ordinary income   A somewhat casual term used in taxes meaning income on which regular taxes are due, without any special consideration. This is in contrast to capital gain taxation which currently has a maximum rate of 28 percent.

Organization for Economic Cooperation and Development (OECD) An international organization that encourages economic growth, high employment, and financial stability among its members. It was an outgrowth of an organization to help Western Europe after World War II. In 1961, it started to extend membership to other nations and today most of the major nations are members.

overtime   Work that is done beyond standard hours which may call for additional compensation, particularly by non-exempt employees. Employees sometimes have the choice of taking time off in lieu of money.

over-the-counter (OTC)   A stock traded without being listed on a stock exchange, but by brokers connected and traded electronically to each other. See NASD and NASDAQ.

par value   The face value of a bond, usually $1,000. Municipal bonds usually have a face value of $5,000. Treasury issues have varying par values.

pawnbroker   Individual or employee of a pawn shop who lends money at a high rate of interest to a borrower leaving collateral such as jewelry, furs, appliances, or other valuable items. If the loan is repaid, the borrower gets the collateral back. If the loan is not repaid, the pawnbroker keeps the collateral, and in many cases, sells it to the public. Borrowers who turn to pawnbrokers and pawn shops typically do not have access to credit from banks or other financial institutions because they are in poor financial condition.

payback period   The amount of time it takes for the money you put into an investment to come back in interest, income or appreciation. The payback period is thus the recovery period for getting your money back.

paycheck withholding   Various items that are deducted from gross pay, such as medical and life insurance, 401(k) deductions, FICA taxes for Social Security, and, of course, state and federal income tax withholding. Sometimes refers only to the income tax withholding.

payout ratio   The percentage of net earnings that a company pays to its investors in the form of dividends. The higher a payout ratio, the less a company has to invest in equipment and other technology.

payroll   The total salaries and wages paid to employees. Salaries are usually deemed to be paid to professionals, while wages are often deemed to be paid to factory workers. However, the color of the money is the same.

pension plan   A retirement fund that pays a benefit at a specific retirement age, usually as a monthly payment. Frequently contributed to by only the company. The usual form of payment is an annuity payment, but some companies offer a lump sum. The law states that if an employee is married, then a 50 percent joint and survivor annuity is to be chosen unless the spouse waives that right, in which case a lump sum can be paid, if offered. Typically, a reduced amount is paid if started before a certain age, for instance age sixty-five or sixty-two.

penny stock   A low priced stock, although rarely actually a penny. Usually more than $1, these stocks are traded on the over-the-counter market and other smaller exchanges.

per diem   Per day. Expense accounts in business are often calculated per diem, meaning that an employee is given a daily allowance for her expenses.

petty cash   A small amount of cash kept available at a company for immediate and miscellaneous expenses, such as some extra baseballs for the company team.

Phillips curve   A relationship between inflation and unemployment written about by economist W.H. Phillips (1914-1975), who postulated that when unemployment is high, inflation is low. When unemployment is low, inflation is high. There have been times where both have been high or low. In the 1970s, inflation soared and unemployment was also high.

planned economy   An economy that is planned and controlled mostly by the government, as opposed to a free market, in which individuals and businesses make most of the economic decisions.

policy   An insurance contract. A life-insurance policy specifies who is insured, the beneficiary, and the various terms of the insurance. A property insurance policy specifies what is covered, which perils are covered, and how much would be paid under what condition.

policy owner   The company or individual who has the right to exercise control over the policy.

portfolio   An investor's total investments.

poverty   The lowest level of individual earnings and assets in a country. It is determined either by a general percentage or by a specific level of earnings per size of households.

precious metals   Gold, silver, and other metals of high value. Mutual funds of precious metals are invested in mining stocks and gold bullion.

preemptive rights   The right of stockholders to purchase additional shares or other securities before they are sold to other purchasers.

preferred stock   A class of stock that has some preference over common stock, usually to receive the dividend first, or receive a dividend at all.

premium   1. The charge for insurance. Premiums are usually paid annually, semi-annually, or quarterly.   2. When a bond's value is greater than par value. When interest rates decline the market value of a bond goes up and is valued at a premium.

prepaid expenses   An expense paid in advance, such as rent. A company may simply have the extra cash or it may want to add to expenses at the end of the accounting period as a way of decreasing its immediate taxes.

price   The amount you are willing to pay as a consumer, and the amount a producer is willing to sell it to you for. See supply and demand.

price/earnings ratio (P/E ratio)   An important investment calculation, the current price of a company's stock divided by the earnings per share. The price/earnings ratio is just that—the ratio of the price of stock to the company's earnings. It is a quick look for investors to see if a stock has been evaluated by the market at higher or lower than other stocks in the same industry.

prime rate   Base rate that banks use in pricing commercial loans to their best and most creditworthy customers. The rate is determined by the Federal Reserve's decision to raise or lower prevailing interest rates for short-term borrowing. Though some banks charge their best customers more and some less than the official prime rate, the rate tends to become standard across the banking industry when a major banks moves its prime up or down. The rate is a key interest rate, since loans to less-creditworthy customers are often tied to the prime rate. For example, a blue-chip company may borrow at a prime rate of 8%, but a less-well-established small business may borrow from the same bank at prime plus 2, or 10%. Many consumer loans, such as home equity, automobile, mortgage, and credit card loans, are tied to the prime rate. Although the major bank prime rate is the definitive "best rate" reference point, many banks, particularly those in outlying regions, have a two-tier system, whereby smaller companies of top-credit standing may borrow at an even lower rate.

PRIMES/SCORES   A PRIME is a unit of investment containing only the income part of the stock, whereas a SCORE is the unit containing the growth or appreciation of the same stock. Thus, a stock has been divided into two so an investor can, if they so choose, receive only one element of that stock. They are limited in number and are traded on the American Stock Exchange.

private sector   That part of the economy made up of businesses and individuals, as opposed to government.

privatization   The process of moving government functions into the private sector. Many cities have privatized the removal of garbage, among other services. The proposed idea of having individuals deposit a part of their Social Security payments into their own private account is termed privatization.

productivity   An amount of output compared to an amount of input. Higher amounts of work per worker suggest more efficient work. If the output of a bookkeeper can increase by using a computer instead of doing handwritten calculations, then that person can do more work per day, and thus is more productive.

program trading   A sophisticated investment strategy of taking an opposite position in futures contracts to one's investments. This is primarily a strategy for a large investor or institutional investment firm, employing computer systems to automatically transact these trades. Program trading was blamed for much of the fall in stock prices in October 1987.

profit   Revenues minus expenses equals profits. It is the money remaining after all the expenses are paid. In economics, it is the incentive to price the products and services high enough to make it worthwhile for producers, but low enough to be afforded by consumers.

profit and loss statement   See income statement.

profit center   A self-contained part of a company that is responsible for its own revenue and expenses, or profits. Usually a separate business unit.

profit-sharing plan   Agreement between a corporation and its employees that allows the employees to share in company profits. Annual contributions are made by the company, when it has profits, to a profit-sharing account for each employee, either in cash or in a deferred plan, which may be invested in stocks, bonds, or cash equivalents. The funds in a profit-sharing account generally accumulate tax deferred until the employee retires or leaves the company. Many plans allow employees to borrow against profit-sharing accounts for major expenditures such as purchasing a home or financing children's education. Because corporate profit-sharing plans have custody over billions of dollars, they are major institutional investors in the stock and bond markets.

progressive tax   An income tax system where the percentage of tax on an individual's income increases as that individual's income increases. For instance, the lowest federal tax rate is 15 percent, the next, 28 percent, then 31 percent, then 36 percent, and eventually 39.6 percent as income exceeds about $265,000. See regressive tax.

proprietary lease   The lease a co-op corporation gives to a co-op apartment owner to allow the owner to live in a specific apartment. The owner's payments cover operating costs and any debt on the complex.

prospectus   1. A legal document made available to potential investors with financial information about the company or mutual fund. 2. A legal document that sets forth the terms of an offering for sale.

proxy   An authority for one person to act in place of another. A company usually solicits proxies from stockholders who do not expect to attend the annual stockholder's meeting.

proxy statement   As a stock holder in a company, you have the right to vote on major decisions that company makes—usually one share, one vote. A proxy statement is an absentee ballot, so you can cast your vote even if you aren't able to make the annual shareholder's meeting in person, which almost no one does.

public (going public)   When a company puts shares in the corporation up for public sale.

pyramiding   A classic illegal investment scheme in which an operator promises very high returns but only distributes money contributed from new investors, while the operator uses and spends most of the money. The schemes don't last long because investors often get worried and demand their money back; it's rarely available.

public spending   Government spending at the federal, state, and local levels.

purchasing power parity (PPP)   The general hypothesis that consumers equally situated in different countries have roughly the same purchasing power.

quotas   Limits placed on the import of certain goods.

rate   The cost of a unit of insurance, which thereby determines the amount of the premium.

rate of return   Although a general term, it usually means the annual percentage return of an investment. It can mean just the interest or dividend of a security, or it can mean the total return, which is the increase or decrease of the investment plus the interest or dividend.

rating services   See AAA, AA, A ratings.

raw materials   Basic minerals and materials usually mined that are used in most manufactured goods. Iron, aluminum, and sand are all raw materials used in many of the products we buy.

recapitalization   A major change or restructuring of the long-term financing mix of a company.

Reaganomics   The general economic policies employed by the Reagan administration, of which cutting taxes was a central tenet. According to Reaganomics, having to pay less in taxes, businesses would produce more, thereby increasing economic growth and creating more jobs.

real income   Income adjusted for inflation. This is in contrast to nominal income, which is in actual dollars.

recession   A technical term applied after two consecutive quarters of decreasing gross domestic product. Usually a recession lasts for a short time, from several months to a year or so. The last recession started, according to this definition, in July 1990 and lasted until March 1991. A related term is depression, which is a significant and prolonged downturn in the economy, the last one being the Great Depression of the 1930s. See depression.

reciprocity   The practice of countries giving each other the same concessions or restrictions.

red-herring prospectus   A preliminary prospectus offered to investors before the price is set and before the SEC has ruled on the prospectus.

redemption fee   A mutual fund fee charged when shares of the fund are sold. Also called deferred sales charge, back-end load, or exit fee.

refund A tax amount returned after overpayment.

regional exchanges Smaller versions of the NYSE and AMEX exchanges. Regional exchanges are located around the country and trade the same stocks as those listed on the NYSE and AMEX. Results of the five regional exchanges are combined with results from the NYSE and AMEX to get a composite trading listing.

regressive tax A tax that is generally flat and applies to most consumers, regardless of income. A sales tax is said to be regressive because everybody has to pay it and it is the same rate for everyone. It doesn't depend on one's income. See progressive tax.

regulation Government rules and supervision, usually through legislation, of various business and financial activities.

reinvestment Shareholders of mutual funds can decide to reinvest the money they earn, take it in cash, or do a little of each.

REIT (Real Estate Investment Trust) A mutual fund of real estate investments. Some only invest in actual real estate while some invest in mortgages only. Some are hybrid, which invest is some of both.

relocation expense The expense of a moving van, transportation, and often real estate expenses incurred when moving to a job in another city. If a company requests the relocation, it usually will pay most, if not all, of the expenses.

rent 1. In economics, the earnings from land, labor, or capital. 2. Money paid for the use of real estate or other property.

rental income Income received from the rental of real estate; it is taxable income offset by certain expenses and depreciation.

repurchase agreement Also called repos, these usually involve banks that hold government securities for a short-term agreement that will pay a current interest rate. The borrower must "repurchase" the securities at the end of the agreement.

residential property Property used for homes, as opposed to commercial or office space. Single-family homes, apartment buildings, and co-ops all fall in this category.

restricted stock Stock given to company executives that does not instantly become fully owned by the executives. It is given as an incentive for the executives to stay with the company. It is restricted because the executive cannot treat it fully as his own, although usually the company will pay the executive the amount of the stock dividend.

retiree That exalted status of not working but receiving a pension and living the good life. Actually refers to just about anyone who leaves a company after from about age fifty-five to sixty-five, whether they receive a pension or not.

retirement counseling A session with a company benefits specialist to complete forms and make benefit decisions at the time an employee is retiring.

retirement planning seminar Sometimes offered by companies for employees over a certain age, the seminar usually covers the essential topics of benefits and how they are taxed, Social Security, investments, insurance, taxes, and estate planning.

retirement plan The government allows an employee and his or her company to put away a certain amount of income to be used after retirement. This income is exempt from taxes until used. If the money is used before retirement, it is subject to penalty fees as well as taxes. Because of their tax advantages—and the impending problems of the Social Security system—retirement plans are very popular.

return A very general term, usually meaning the profit made from an investment.

return on investment (ROI) A traditional and important calculation made by taking the net profits, after taxes, divided by the total assets of a company. It is sometimes called the profitability ratio, because it shows the ability of the company's assets to generate profits. It is sometimes also called return on assets.

revenue Income from an investment or production. Revenue also refers to the taxes that the government collects.

revenue bonds State bonds backed by the revenue, or income, from a specific source, such as tolls on bridges and tunnels. They are considered riskier than general obligation bonds and therefore often have insurance to back up the risk.

reverse annuity mortgage (RAM) A mortgage specifically designed for older homeowners who have little, if any, outstanding debt on their homes. In this mortgage, you are essentially borrowing against the value of your home and receiving a monthly payment from the bank. At some point, usually when the house is sold or upon the death of the mortgage holder, the note is due. The longer the note is held, the more money is due to the bank.

risk A widely used and important aspect of investments to measure the uncertainty of an investment. Technically, professional investors use the statistical measure of one standard deviation as the measurement of risk. The general concept in the world of finance and investment is: The greater the risk the greater the potential gain of an investment (or loss). High-risk investments may be a big gamble, but they lure investors with a possible high return.

rollover IRA   An IRA created at the time of receiving a lump sum distribution from your 401(k) plan or pension plan. The lump sum is then put into an IRA called a rollover IRA.

rollover mortgage   A mortgage in which every few years—or whatever time specified—the mortgage amount is technically due, yet the lender carries over the amount to a new mortgage with a new interest rate. May also be called a renewable mortgage.

Russell 2000/3000   Two useful indexes of smaller cap stocks. The Russell 2000 consists of smaller capitalization stocks. It generally represents companies with a market value of $250 million or less. The Russell 3000 consists of the largest 3,000 publicly traded stocks of U.S. domiciled corporations and includes both large, medium and small capitalization stocks. It represents about 98 percent of the total capitalization of the New York, American and NASDAQ market.

S&P 500   See Standard & Poor's.

Salamon Brothers bond index   An overall index of fixed-income securities that combines U.S. treasury and agency securities, corporate bonds, and mortgage-backed securities.   The index is considered a good combination of index considering both income and price fluctuation.   The index is approximately 55 percent U.S. treasuries, 20 percent Corporate, and 25 percent Mortgage-backed securities.

salary   The compensation received for work. The term salary originally comes from the Latin word for salt, which is what Roman soldiers were paid in, as it was so scarce at the time.

salary reduction plans   Plans such as 401(k) and 403(b) that allow pre-tax contributions. This means that you don't pay taxes on the money that is contributed, thus lowering your taxes. Your taxable salary is reduced by the amount of money contributed to the plans.

sales tax   A state tax on certain purchases; a percentage of the total price of taxable items.

savings   Amounts of money and investments that individuals set aside each year to build up their financial reserves. Savings are the amount left over after taxes and expenses.

savings and loan   See bank failure.

savings bonds (EE and HH bonds)   See EE and HH bonds.

second mortgage   The mortgage that takes second place behind a main or first mortgage. It is an additional mortgage on a property, often a credit-line home loan for a homeowner.

secondary market   Stocks and bonds traded after they are offered initially. Even though the New York Stock Exchange and other exchanges provide for initial offerings called IPOs (initial public offerings), the exchanges are primarily a place to trade these shares on a continual basis, called the secondary market.

secondary mortgage market   Banks often sell their mortgages to government and private agencies in order to have more cash on hand to extend new mortgages.

secondary offering   If a public company wants to raise additional money, they may issue a secondary offering, which is another chunk of stock.

securities   Stocks or bonds.

Securities and Exchange Commission (SEC)   A government watchdog agency that regulates the investment industry. Created in 1934, the SEC makes sure that investors are properly informed about their investments and that transactions are fair and free from fraud. It also investigates alleged wrong doing, such as illegal insider trading.

seed money   Money needed to start a real estate venture—usually for land, legal advice, and market study.

selling short against the box   A maneuver by an investor who owns a number of shares in a particular stock and although wants to keep them is worried that the price of the stock may drop. The investor could sell the shares, but would incur immediate capital gains on those shares. The investor could also sell borrowed stock, called short selling, or selling short. Now, if the stock does go down, the investor could buy shares at a lower price to replace the sold shares, bought low and sold high, although in reverse. If the stock does go up, then the investor has the original shares to replace the borrowed ones that were sold.

SEP (simplified employee pension)   An IRA plan set up in conjunction with your company that is simplified relative to the more complex pension or 401(k)-type plan. It's an easy plan to administer and is primarily for self-employed people and their employees. These plans are sometimes referred to as SEP-IRAs.

SERP (Supplementary Executive Retirement Plan)   An additional pension amount for executives to make up for the pensions disallowed because of government regulations. The plans are allowed but do not have any favored tax treatment, in that all payments are ordinary income.

severance package   A potential variety of services when a person is downsized or rightsized. It could include outplacement, an office with a phone, and additional compensation called severance pay.

severance pay   Pay offered to an employee after he or she has been fired.

share   One unit of company ownership, through a stock certificate.

shareholder   See stockholder.

sharp ratio   A measurement of the riskiness of a stock or mutual fund. It is a somewhat crude measurement of the expected or past return above treasury interest divided by the standard deviation of the stock or mutual fund. The greater the standard deviation, or risk, the lower the sharp ratio.

short selling   An investment strategy that at first look seems either illegal or contorted, although it's perfectly legal; however, it may be confusing. First you borrow shares from a broker and sell them. Then you hope the price drops. When it does then you buy back the same shares at a lower price and return the newly purchased shares back to your broker. Everyone is happy, especially you because you've made a profit. It's a backward way to make money; you sell first, then buy. Of course this strategy doesn't work if the price of the shares goes up. See uptick rule and technical analysis.

short-term capital gain or loss   A gain, or loss, on an investment or asset held for one year or less. Any asset held for longer than one year is called a long-term capital gain or loss.

silver certificates   United States dollars printed before 1963 were backed by silver reserves. Silver certificates are collector's items today, even though they can no longer be traded for silver.

simple interest   Calculation based only on the original principal amount. Simple interest contrasts with compound interest, which is applied to principal plus accumulated interest. For example, $100 on deposit at 12% simple interest would yield $12 per year (12% of $100). The same $100 at 12% interest compounded annually would yield $12 only in the first year. The second year's inte amount of cash, or undervalued real estate or other assets.

single-country fund   A sector mutual fund that invests only in a single country, such as Japan or Spain. Investors who believe that special circumstances prevail in a country can try to take advantage of it through a fund that specializes in it.

sinking fund A cash reserve set aside for bonds to pay the eventual par value at maturity.

small-cap fund small-cap stocks The term cap stands for capitalization, meaning a small company with fewer than average shares and often with less than average earnings. Picking the right small-cap stocks can mean significant investment returns. See large-cap fund/stocks.

smart cards Plastic cards used primarily in situations where change is needed—vending machines and the like. The amount is automatically debited from the card each time you use it.

social investing socially responsible investing Also called conscience or green funds, these investments are designed for investors who want to invest with a social conscience. They generally shun companies that are not "politically correct" or that have poor environmental records.

Social Security A governmental system of paying a basic pension to those who are of a certain age. Most countries have such a system, including the United States. Contributions are made from your paycheck into the system while you are working, and then you receive payments when retired. Money does not go into a fund, but is paid out to those who are retired. This is called a pay-as-you-go system. Only Chile is experimenting with a system where employees' money goes into their own accounts.

Social Security tax A tax withheld from a paycheck to finance the Social Security system (primarily for retirees and disabled people). Social Security, with the Medicare tax, is part of the FICA tax withheld from a paycheck.

Socialism A social and economic system where the production of goods and delivery of services are collectively owned by everyone in the society. It requires strong government intervention and control of industries. This is in contrast to capitalism, in which individuals own the means of own production.

soft market Characterized by an excess of supply over demand. A soft market in securities is marked by inactive trading, wide bid-offer spreads, and pronounced price drops in response to minimal selling pressure. Also called buyer's market.

specialist A member of the stock exchange who maintains an orderly market for specific stocks. He "specializes" in those stocks. He also buys and sells those stocks for his own portfolio to maintain an orderly market.

speculator One who invests in risky financial transactions, not just your average investor. Investments may take the form of highly risky stock or unusual transactions like speculating in a currency devaluation.

split See stock split.

split-dollar insurance An agreement between a company and its executives to share in the cost of life insurance and a sharing by the company of the eventual insurance payout.

spread In stock markets, the difference between the highest price a buyer asks and the lowest price a seller offers. In the futures market, the spread is the difference between a sell contract and a buy contract on a commodity. When you play around with options, the spread is when you buy and write options for the same commodity at the same time. In all these cases, the spread will dictate how much money an investor makes in a deal.

Standard & Poor's; Standard & Poor's 500 Standard & Poor's is an investment advisory service that publishes financial information. For the stock market it publishes the 500 index which is a widely-used index by professional investors as a gauge of the stock market as a whole. It contains the 500 largest capitalized stocks in the United States, and as such it contains so many companies that it is considered the best overall measurement of the stock market. The Dow Jones Industrial Average consists only of 30 stocks. Capitalization is measured by the price of a company's stock multiplied by the number of outstanding shares.

statement of cash flows A key financial report that shows the sources and uses of the company's cash flows over a specific period of time. It can be called by a variety of names, for example, statement of sources and applications of funds, or statement of changes in net working capital. Sometimes it is simply called the funds statement.

stock One unit of ownership in a company. It is the capital a company raises by selling shares. Stock also refers to the certificate that shows ownership of shares. The terms stock and share are interchangeable.

stock buyback A company's buying of its own stock on the open market. There are several reasons why a company would do this: Sometimes to make it harder for the company to be taken over by another company, sometimes to increase the price of the remaining stock, and sometimes because a company has excess cash and feels there is no better alternative use for the money.

stock dividends   A dividend paid as additional common stock rather than in cash.

stock exchange   A place where stocks and securities are bought and sold.

stock market   The general term for the market of common stock on the various stock exchanges.

stock options   A common executive compensation practice of providing an option to buy stock at a certain price in the future. If the stock goes up, then the executive can exercise those options at the lower price and reap the rewards. There are generally two types of options, ISOs (incentive stock options) and NQSOs (non-qualified stock options). The first has special tax benefits while the second is treated as ordinary income when exercised.

stock right   A right to purchase a prescribed number of shares at a predetermined price.

stock split   If the price of a share of stock gets too high, the company may split the stock. Investors don't make any money on this transaction, although in the long term the company, and investors, believe that the stock will go up more. A two for one split will immediately result in twice as many shares at one-half the price.

stockholder   An owner of shares of stock in a company, sometimes called a shareholder.

stockholder's equity   What the owner's of a company own. That is, the sum total of all outstanding stock, common and preferred shares, and retained earnings. It's what the accountants tell us is left over after liabilities.

stop-loss order   An order telling a broker to sell a stock if it falls to a certain price. It is usually placed by an investor who suspects that the price may drop. A stop-loss order may be good 'til canceled (GTC) or a day order.

straddle   Buying a combination of put and call options. Investors look for volatile stock and try straddles, to make money one way or another.

straight-line depreciation   A method of depreciation in which an equal portion of an asset's cost is written off each year. See depreciation.

strong dollar   See dollar is higher/lower.

summer rally   A general upward trend on stock markets during the summertime. It is thought that during the summer there is often less negative news to cause the market to drop.

supply The production and introduction of products and services. It is the willingness on the part of businesses and individuals to offer goods and services to consumers. This is one side of supply and demand. Demand is our desire for specific products and services tempered by our ability to pay for them. Supply is the offering of goods by businesses and individuals.

supply and demand The basic economic concept that prices affect what you buy. In general, the lower the price, the more you will want to buy, which is the demand. The higher the price the more the producer will want to sell, which is the supply. The price that is just right, balances the supply and demand and is called the equilibrium price.

supply-side economics The economic philosophy of cutting taxes on individuals and business so there will be greater stimulus to produce more goods and services. Although taxes are a starting point, the object of cutting taxes is to stimulate the economy by having more money available to purchase a greater supply of goods and services. Thus, the philosophy begs the question: will businesses produce more when consumers have more money? See demand-side economics.

swap An agreement by two parties to exchange a series of cash flows, for example fixed-rate payments for floating-rate payments.

tangibles An investment that is real that you can actually touch, such as real estate or gold. This is opposed to intangible investments such as stocks and bonds, which are only paper representations.

tape The band of stock quotations that move along at the bottom of a news cable channel, or on a computer screen, showing each trade on the stock exchanges. At one time the ticker-tape machines clicked away at brokerage offices, and provided the fodder for New York City ticker-tape parades. Now we have computers and no more strips of ticker-tape for the parades.

tax abatement An official reduction or complete suspension of real estate taxes after the initial assessment has been made on a property.

tax audit An IRS notice that they think you owe more taxes than you indicated. Don't panic. If it is complicated, get yourself a competent tax professional to help; if it's simple, you can represent yourself. Gather your information and present it to the IRS in a logical and professional way.

tax break   Anything that allows one to pay less in taxes. Deductions and exemptions are examples of tax breaks.

tax deferred annuities (TDAs)   Sometimes called 403(b) plans, they are typically a defined contribution plan available to teachers, hospitals, and nonprofit organizations. However, an organization must sponsor such a plan, as contributions are through payroll deductions. Once sponsored, then employees generally are able to select from several insurance companies the one that is to receive their contributions. The contributions are almost always pretax.

tax exempt; tax-free bonds; tax-free mutual fund   An investment in which the interest earned by it is not taxed. These are municipal bonds and are offered by most states, cities, and many counties. If you live in the state in which it is offered, then it is usually tax exempt on your federal and state income tax, otherwise out-of-state bonds are only tax exempt on your federal tax return. In high-tax states, there are usually a number of mutual funds of tax-exempt bond funds for that state.

tax-free   Some income sources are tax-free, in particular tax-free municipal bond interest. However, some tax-free munis, as they are called for short, have some AMT taxes that may be owed, and believe it or not, some tax-free municipals are actually taxable.

tax roll   The list of people or companies who pay property tax in a given municipality.

tax sale   The sale of property to pay property taxes.

tax software   Specialized software that helps individuals and businesses fill out their federal and state tax returns; some programs help with tax planning as well. Some popular tax software for individuals is Tax Cut and Turbo Tax.

taxable income   Income subject to tax after subtracting all allowable deductions. Gifts and inheritances are generally tax-free when received, although the income from them will be taxable when earned.

taxes   Payments to federal, state, and local governments, for government expenditures. Taxes come in many forms, such as income, sales, and estate taxes.

technical analysis   One of two approaches to analyzing the stock market. Technical analysis relies primarily on market volume or price movements to determine the best time to buy or sell stocks. This is opposed to fundamental analysis, which analyzes business earnings, balance sheets, and economic factors of a particular company or its business sector to determine if a stock, or group of stocks, should be bought or sold. See fundamental analysis.

tenant   Someone who occupies property, but does not own it.

term life insurance   See life insurance.

tight money   The monetary policy of the Federal Reserve (Fed) to make less money available in the economy in hopes of slowing down an overly stimulated economy. The opposite of the Fed's easy or loose money policy.

title   Proof of ownership. In real estate, title is exchanged at the closing. The title must be clear of all outstanding liens before it is passed on.

title insurance   Protection sold as insurance that the title is actually valid and that only the owner has claim to the property.

trade secret   A proprietary process or formula used in a business that is unique. It is given certain legal rights; however, it is not a patent, which is disclosed when applied for.

trader   The people who actually execute the buy and sell orders. Traders must be registered, and they charge a fee for making the trade.

trading pit   The area on the floor of an exchange in which the trading takes place. A pit may be divided into areas for different types of trades.

transfer payment   Referring to a payment, such as a welfare payment, to someone in a society from the government. It is a redistribution from the general society to individuals.

treasury direct   An account established to buy and hold Treasury bonds directly through the Federal Reserve Bank. No brokers to talk to and no commission to pay. A do-it-yourself investment. The account is usually established with a bank so everything can be done electronically, interest is automatically deposited into the account.

trickle-down economics   An economic theory, and practice, that promotes the general economy, at the expense of government support for needy people, in anticipation that as the economy does well, so will lower income citizens. The benefits thus "trickle-down" to all people.

triple A   A bond that is rated with three As, as in AAA. See AAA rating.

trustee/trustor   In legal talk, the person who holds/the person who creates the trust. That is, a person who holds or manages the money to a trust is the trustee, while the person who created and contributed to the trust is the trustor.

trusts A legal entity that allows for the accumulation or payment of money to specified people under specified circumstances. Parents often set up a trust in their will, for example, in case they both die while their children are still minors. The trust specifies how and when the money is to be distributed to the children.

T-bills; T-notes; T-bonds Treasury securities of different maturities. T-bills are issued from three months to one year, T-notes are issued from two years to ten years, and T-bonds are issued for twenty and thirty years.

umbrella policy A policy giving an extra liability insurance with regular insurance.

undercapitalized A company or enterprise that does not have enough capital to carry out its business.

underlying investment When purchasing an option, the actual security that the option allows you to buy. The underlying investment is the security itself, not the option.

underwrite; underwriter; underwriting A brokerage firm, or firms, assuming the financial responsibility for new securities by buying them from the issuer and then selling them to the broker's clients. Thus, the brokerage firm guarantees to the issuer they will receive the funds needed from the new securities.

undeveloped country A country whose economy is poorly developed. More commonly referred to as a less developed country, or LDC for short.

unearned income Income from sources other than salary, wages, or tips. It is generally from investments.

unemployment Having no work, but being able and willing to work.

uninsured motorist coverage Auto insurance coverage that pays benefits if the motorist who caused the accident does not have insurance.

U.S. Savings bonds See EE and HH bonds.

utility The amount of psychic gratification, desirability, or need consumers get from goods and services. Because people get satisfaction from goods and services, we demand them. That demand, however, is usually tempered by our being more and more satisfied after using the goods and services. Thus the demand usually decreases on the margin, or after each use. The term marginal utility refers to this diminished satisfaction of consumers after each use. Some products or services tend to have an increasing demand at the margin, such as potato chips or cigarettes.

utilities   Public services, such as water, gas, electricity, and telephone.

value added tax (VAT)   A form of tax especially popular in Europe, where governments tax each step of the production process, at each step where value is added. The tax is on the value added.

value stocks   See growth versus value.

variable costs   Any cost that changes proportionately in relation to output.

variable interest   rate Interest rate on a loan that rises and falls based on the movement of an underlying index of interest rates. For example, many credit cards charge variable interest rates, based on a specific spread over the prime rate. Most home equity loans charge variable rates tied to the prime rate. Also called adjustable interest rates.

variable   rate mortgage See adjustable rate mortgage (ARM).

velocity of money   The speed at which money circulates in an economy.

venture capital   Money for new businesses, usually smaller riskier businesses. Since getting a bank loan for many startup businesses is out of the question from conservative-minded banks, investors turn to venture capitalists who may lend money to the fledgling enterprise.

vesting   An important term to know, it's when you are officially at your company long enough to be entitled to a benefit. For instance, you may have to be at your company five years to be entitled to a pension plan. Not to be confused with the normal one-year rule before you can start to contribute to a 401(k) plan. Although you are always entitled to your own contributions, frequently the company contributions to the 401(k), assuming the company is contributing, are only yours after working for a few years. When the company contributions can be yours usually takes one of three general forms of vesting.

volatility   When a stock, or the market itself, experiences large swings in prices it is said to be volatile. The opposite is a stable, or boring market. Active investors and speculators like volatile markets for the potential price swings and potential profits to be made.

voodoo economics   A general term applied to economic theories or practices that are considered odd or unworkable. First used by George Bush when he was running against Ronald Reagan. He called Reagan's economic plans "voodoo economics."

wages Pay. Minimum wage set by union and federal legislation is called the wage floor. If wages will not be increased for a set period, that is called a wage freeze.

Wall Street 1. Common name for the financial district at the lower end of Manhattan in New York City, where the New York and American Stock Exchanges and numerous brokerage firms are headquartered. The New York Stock Exchange is actually located at the corner of Wall and Broad Streets. 2. Investment community, such as in "Wall Street really likes the prospects for that company" or "Wall Street law firm," meaning a firm specializing in securities law and mergers. Also referred to as "the Street."

Wall Street Journal The popular daily newspaper of business and investments.

wallpaper Worthless securities. The implication of the term is that certificates of stocks and bonds that have gone bankrupt or defaulted have no other use than as wallpaper. However, there may be value in the worthless certificates themselves by collectors of such certificates, who prize rare or historically significant certificates. The practice of collecting such certificates is known as scripophily.

warrants A security that allows you the right to buy the company's common stock at a predetermined price by a certain date. For instance, a company may offer a warrant that gives the investor the right to purchase shares of stock at $25 up until December 31, 1999.

weak dollar See dollar is higher/lower

welfare state A term used to indicate widespread use of government programs for the poor in a society.

whole life insurance A form of life insurance where cash values are accrued as well as pure life insurance. Thus, a whole life policy is both a vehicle for investment and insurance. Sometimes whole life is called permanent life insurance, however, a policy holder can stop it anytime, so it really isn't permanent.

widget Symbolic American gadget, used wherever a hypothetical product is needed to illustrate a manufacturing or selling concepts.

will A written document specifying who is to get what at a person's death. Generally, it is known as the last will and testament. Technically the term will means the giving of real property, like real estate, and the term testament refers to personal property.

Wilshire 4500/5000 Two useful indexes of all U.S. stocks. The

Wilshire 5000 consists of all domestic stocks of the United States, while the Wilshire 4500 consists of all stocks except the largest 500, which is the S&P 500. The Wilshire 4500 represents about 30 percent of the entire stock market with the S&P 500 being about 70 percent. (There are about 6,000 actual individual stocks at anyone time combined in all of the markets).

wire house   A casual name for a large brokerage firm. The names comes from the past when the firms received confirmation of stock market trades by wire from the floor.

withholding   A portion of income taken out of a paycheck for various taxes or employee plans. Withholding is used for income taxes, Social Security taxes, 401(k) plans, and the like.

working capital   The excess of current assets over current liabilities. Also called net working capital.

workers compensation   A state system of medical and disability coverage for on-the-job accidents and illness. Each state has differing coverage, different rules, and different rates. Companies pay the premiums.

World Bank   Created by the Bretton Woods agreement in 1944, it lends money to countries who have difficulty getting loans from private sources. The more developed countries contribute funds to the bank. The bank is more formally called the International Bank for Reconstruction and Development. See Bretton Woods.

wrap-around account   A brokerage account where the firm offers a named professional investor that will provide the investment advice for the individual's account.

wraparound mortgage   A mortgage that is added to and includes an old mortgage. In a wraparound mortgage, the new lender will assume the obligation to pay off the old mortgage.

Yankee bond   Bonds sold by foreign bond issuers to American investors that are denominated in dollars, rather than their own foreign currency. This eliminates the uncertainty of currency fluctuations for the American investor.

yield   The income earned on an investment, either interest as in a bond or dividend as in a stock.

yield curve   A chart showing the current treasury interest rates for different maturities. It is a curved line starting with short-term interest rates on the three-month treasury bill continuing all the way out to the thirty-year treasury bond. It represents to investors the current risk-free investment yields at any maturity.

yield to maturity The total return on a bond to the maturity date on the bonds. If an investor bought the bonds either at a premium (bond was higher than par) or at a discount (bond was lower than par), that decrease or increase to par at maturity is calculated along with the interest earned to maturity to give a true total return of the bond.

zero-based budgeting (ZBB) A method of budgeting in which each activity or project is evaluated anew each year. This is in contrast to the practice of adding an incremental increase to budgets. It allows a fresh look at ongoing business activities.

zero-coupon bonds A bond that pays no current interest, but instead pays it all when it matures. Thus, an investor buys the bond at a discount and increases in value until it matures.

Appendix

Taxes

When it comes to doing your taxes for the annual April 15th dead-line, here are two recommendations. Explore the marvels of the new computer software programs like TurboTax, the market leader. These personal tax programs are as significant a development for professional tax preparers as the ATM was for banking, and now you have access to them.

If you have a fairly straightforward return, take a shot at com-pleting the form yourself. The instructions on the new forms are easier to understand than the older forms, and there are toll-free numbers to call for help. However, if you have a complicated return—and this is the second recommendation—consider getting professional help. Some tax experts feel returns that have been professionally prepared discourage audits later. Regardless, it's usually well worth the piece of mind.

According to Ray Martin, the best thing you can do is to prepare well ahead of the April 15th deadline. Here are his other suggestions:

- *Take full advantage of your company's savings plan or an IRA.* These are some of the best ways to protect your income from taxes while building a nest egg for retirement.

- *Keep precise records.* Poor record keeping not only makes the process difficult, it may keep you from taking advantage of important tax breaks. For instance, if you donated all of your clothes and furniture from college to the Salvation Army, keep the receipt with the estimated value of your contribution in a safe place. It could be a significant tax deduction for you.

- *Withhold enough from your paycheck.* The accounting department at work can tell you if enough money is being withheld for taxes from each paycheck. It's much better to have too much (the government will refund it to you) than too little withheld and have to pay more money come April 15th.

- *Take advantage of any dependent-care or health-care spending accounts available through your employer.* If you estimate your spending correctly, these accounts nearly always work to your advantage.

- *File on time.* Unless there are circumstances beyond your control, file by (and preferably, before) the April 15th deadline. Yes, you can apply for an extension, but if you owe taxes, interest penalties will be assessed.

How To Buy A Car

Almost everyone has to buy a car at some point. How much do you really know about the process? After all, how hard is it to go into a showroom, kick some tires, and start negotiating with the dealer? In fact, the decision to buy a car is much more complicated. It is the most expensive purchase you'll make next to buying a home or financing a college education. And car-related expenses—gas, maintenance, and insurance—can take a big bite out of your wallet. Here are some pointers on how to get the best deal you can with the least amount of pain.

1. How much can you afford?

Know your limits and what you should be spending. You may be inclined to take whatever money you have after paying your rent and bills, and use this to buy a car. That's not a sound approach. You shouldn't spend more than 10 percent of your gross income on car expenses—this includes the cost of the car along with insurance, gas, and maintenance. For example, if you make $25,000, your car allowance shouldn't be more than $2,500. Realize that everything is negotiable—not just the price of the car. From the floor mats to the interest rate on your loan payments, all the extras are negotiable too.

2. How to choose the right type of car.

Once you know how much you can afford to pay for a car, you have to do some serious thinking about what type of car to buy and what features are important to you. For example, you should know which options you'll really use. If you live in New England, you need a rear-window defroster. If you park in the city at night, you may not want a fancy CD player that could be stolen easily.

You want to buy a car that you really need, not one you simply want, and you should evaluate those needs and wants before you go to a dealer. Otherwise, a highly trained salesperson may persuade you to buy a car that's not right for you.

Before going to the dealer, you should:

- Look at consumer magazines such as *Consumer Reports*. They explain what models are rated best for reliability, maintenance costs, safety, fuel economy, and insurance rates.

- See if your credit union offers Autofax. This service provides information on prices, safety records, mileage, etc.

- Make a preliminary choice. Decide on the type and style of car that best suits your needs, and your pocketbook.

- Narrow the field. Choose specific makes and models in your price range.

- Decide on the equipment. What kind of standard equipment and what extras do you want?

It is also important to get a sense of how much your current car is worth so that you can consider a trade-in offer. There are several ways to find this information:

- Use a used-car price service. Auto Price Line, (900) 999-2277, is a hotline that gives prices on used cars and trucks in your state. The cost is $1.75 for the first minute plus 75 cents for each additional minute. *Consumer Reports* Used Car Service, (900) 446-0500, available from 7 a.m. to 2 p.m. EST, seven days a week, charges $1.75 a minute (a typical call lasts five minutes) and provides regional resale prices for any vehicle made from 1985 to 1993.

- Consult the latest copy of the National Automobile Dealers Association (NADA) monthly *Official Used Car Guide*. Also known as the *Blue Book*, it is available at many banks, credit unions, car dealers, and libraries.

- Review Edmund's *Used Car Guide*. It costs about $5, is published quarterly, and is available on newsstands or by mail from Edmund's, 515 Hempstead Turnpike, West Hempstead, NY   11552.

- Check local classifieds. Look at the advertised prices of similar car models. Remember, though, that you'll have to spend some time and effort if you choose to sell your car privately.

3. How to formulate a strategy.

Now you're ready to go to the dealer, and you should know the psychology of salespeople because they certainly know yours. The best thing you can do is show the dealer that you're prepared. Say, "I know what I want to spend, and I want a car with the following options. Let's work out something." If the dealer starts to talk about something else, you should simply say, "You'll need to work within my limits, or I'll have to look elsewhere." Good salespeople will respect and stick with you. If they try to uproot you from your decision, they probably have another agenda. They may be more concerned with getting a bonus or a higher commission for selling you a more expensive car.

Never walk into a car dealer and volunteer what you're able to afford. Once you tell the salesperson a dollar figure, you're far more likely to drive away with a car in the upper range of your budget when you might have gotten something for less.

Don't make snap decisions, regardless of what the salespeople say about special, onetime offers. You're making a significant purchase, and you should definitely wait a minimum of twenty-four hours, although waiting two or three days is even better. There is no deal so sweet that you can't wait it out to deliberate.

After you've been to one dealer, you should visit or call several others to get information and compare prices. After all, the price of a car can vary by hundreds of dollars from one deal to another.

When you call other dealers, pressure them to give you specifics on the phone before you agree to come in. Always ask for the name of the person you talk to, and write down any prices that he or she tells you. And even if you're interested in trading in your current car, never commit over the phone to a trade-in deal.

Here are the most important strategies to use at the dealer:

- Find out how much the dealer is paying for models you're interested in. You can get this information from an industry publication such as the *Kelley Blue Book* and *Automobile Invoice Service*, usually available at local libraries. As a general rule, the dealer expects to make a profit of 5 or 6 percent over invoice. If you drive a hard bargain, you should be able to get a new car for 3 percent over invoice. Try bargaining up from the dealer's cost, not down from the sticker price on the car.

- Find out about any incentives or rebates that might lower your cost. Read the "Incentive Watch" column in the weekly trade publication *Automotive News*, available at libraries and credit unions.

- Watch out for dealer add-ons. "Protection packages," "conveyance fees," and "dealer prep" are just a few. Make sure these items are included in the negotiated price. Don't fall for dealers who insist that you need features such as rustproofing and fabric conditioning.

- Ask about last year's models. Are any still available at a reduced price?

- Anticipate your insurance costs. Consider spending extra money for safety features such as an airbag. Some insurance companies will reduce rates in most states by 25 percent for cars with a driver's-side airbag. Other companies offer similar discounts for passive restraints. Another safety feature worth considering is an anti-lock brake system (ABS).

- Select the best deal in your price range. You may find that the first couple of choices are priced higher than you can afford, even after you subtract trade-in, rebates, and discounts, so be ready with backup choices. The car you finally select may be your second or third choice, but it may save you hundreds of dollars, even when you include all the equipment you want.

- Shop near the end of the month. Before Christmas, or after June are also good times to look. These are times when dealers are struggling to reach sales quotas. The worst time to buy is from March through June when people begin planning summer vacations.

- Take the cash rebate. If your car dealer offers you a choice between a cash rebate and a low-interest-rate loan, you usually are better off taking the cash rebate. You will have to check the numbers, but if you apply the rebate to the down payment and get your own loan, you are borrowing less, which could save you hundreds of dollars in interest payments.

- Ask how long the dealer has been in the same location. This is a good way to separate the legitimate dealers from the fly-by-night operations. The ideal dealer is one who has been in the same location for at least five or six years.

- Keep all your transactions separate. Trading in or selling your old car, financing the new car, and negotiating the new car's price are separate decisions. Each should be conducted independently.

- Keep the deal simple. Don't discuss trade-ins or financing until you have a firm price.

- Be prepared to walk away. If you don't get the deal you want, don't be afraid to walk away.

4. How to pay for your car.

Paying cash for your car is your best move. Cash enables you to avoid paying interest which, of course, can add up to hundreds, even thousands, of dollars over a five-year period. Chances are, however, that you will have to take out some type of financing. You have several options:

- Private bank loan. You should shop at your local home-town bank for a car loan. The interest rates will still be lower—possibly as much as one percentage point—that the loan rate available at the car dealer. That's because the bank is holding onto your loan; a dealer will have to hire a financing agency.

- Car dealership. Borrowing from the dealer where you're buying a car is convenient and, especially if you're buying your first car, it may be the only way you can borrow money. Generally, car dealers have less restrictive credit requirements than banks do. However, be wary of cut-rate financing deals that dealers frequently push. These attractive 3 percent interest rates may apply only to certain models or short-term loans of up to twelve months.

- Generally, car loans feature terms of two, five, or seven years. The type of loan you choose is determined by how much you can afford to pay per month. The lower the monthly payment, the longer the term of the loan. You also have to consider how long you expect your a car to last. If you maintain your call well, it should last you four or five years. Generally, you shouldn't take out a car loan for more than five years, because your car could be falling apart while you're still making payments!

- If you find you can't afford to buy a new car comfortably, don't. Your other options are to buy a used car (many dealers now carry "previously owned" cars that look new and may even carry the balance of the original warranty) or "fix up" your current car.

- Finally, you may wonder why we've not brought up the subject of leasing a new car. Generally speaking, the advantages of leasing for a first-time car buyer, or someone just starting out, do not outweigh the disadvantages. If the concept of leasing still appeals to you, do your homework on this before making any commitments. Most of the time when you do a side-by-side price comparison, buying comes out ahead.

Used with permission from *Your Financial Guide* by Ray Martin (Macmillian, 1996)

The Other Side: Tips From The Dealer

Hollywood has done quite a number on the image of the automobile salesperson. Sometimes the image holds true, but most often it does not, according to Andy Huey, president of Huey Honda in St. Louis. Here are his suggestions for buying a new car:

1. Do your homework. On the Internet or at the library, there is a ton of information about which new cars are best. Also be sure to get a sense of what the interest rates are running.

2. Don't be defensive. The stereotypical salesperson is a thing of the past. The vast majority are looking for a long-term relationship with you; they understand that a satisfied customer is going to (1) recommend the dealer to friends, (2) have the car serviced there, and (3) buy their next car from the same place.

3. You don't have to work with the first sales person who approaches you. If you feel a salesperson is too pushy or simply is not understanding your needs, ask for someone else or for the manager.

4. Don't let the pressure get to you. Even if you have to ride the bus for a few more days, take the time to make the right decision. If you feel rushed, you won't be happy ten minutes after you've driven off the lot.

5. Work with a certified sales person. The new breed of car salesperson are now certified by the National Automobile Dealers Association (NADA) and must adhere to a strict code of ethics. If a complaint is registered, NADA investigates and may impose sanctions against the dealer. Additionally, to be certified a salesperson has to meet product knowledge requirements, attend ethics classes, understand contract law, and know state laws pertaining to purchasing an automobile.

How To Buy A Home

If you're a first-time home buyer, you've undoubtedly heard horror stories from friends about their experiences. Buying a home is simply a bewildering experience that takes on a life of its own. From finding the perfect house to the closing, almost anything can and will happen. Even if your financing comes through without a snag and both you and the seller are reasonable people, assume that some hassles will occur before you move in. Obviously, the more knowledgeable and prepared you are, the more capable you will be in minimizing any problems. Here are the basics:

1. Decide How Much Home You Can Afford.

This is a crucial first question for anyone buying a home. Only you can answer this question. And your response is not how much you will be able to borrow. Don't let a banker or mortgage broker make this decision for you. Remember, you have to consider not just the purchase price, but the additional expenses you'll have as a home owner.

The experts say that you can afford to put 28 percent of your annual income toward housing expenses. In other words, according to the banks, your monthly mortgage principal and interest payments—plus property taxes and home owner's insurance (PITI)—should not exceed 28 percent of your gross monthly income. And your monthly house payment plus other debt should not be more than 36 percent of your annual income. If your job is very secure and your finances are generally in good shape, you can go slightly higher than the 28 percent. The following table gives some examples of annual gross income, monthly gross income, and the amount of this monthly income available for your house payment according to lenders standards.

How Much Can You Afford?

Annual Gross Income	Monthly Gross Income	28% of Monthly Gross Income
$15,000	$1,250	$ 350
$20,000	$1,667	$ 467
$25,000	$2,083	$ 583
$30,000	$2,500	$ 700
$35,000	$2,917	$ 817
$40,000	$3,333	$ 933
$45,000	$3,750	$1,050
$50,000	$4,167	$1,167

Once you know how much you can spend on your monthly house payment, you are on your way to finding out how much you can afford. And the amount you can afford will depend directly upon the interest rate. For instance, you'll be able to buy a more expensive home if you're paying 9 percent interest as opposed to 11 percent.

Mortgage Factors

Annual Mortgage Term			
Interest Rate	15 Years	20 Years	30 Years
4%	135.2	165.0	209.5
5%	126.5	151.5	186.5
6%	118.5	139.6	166.8
7%	111.3	129.0	150.3
8%	104.6	120.0	136.3
9%	98.6	111.1	124.3
10%	93.1	103.6	114.0
11%	88.0	96.9	105.0
12%	83.3	90.8	97.2

2. Review Your Credit Before You Apply For A Mortgage.

By looking at your credit report ahead of time, you'll have no surprises when you fall in love with that perfect house and want to move fast to make it yours. To get a copy of your credit report, call one of the leading credit bureaus: Equifax, (800) 685-1111, or Experian (formerly called TRW), (800) 682-7654. There may be things you can do that will help you qualify for a mortgage. For instance, cancel any inactive credit cards that are open. If any inaccurate information appears on your report, write the credit bureaus and explain the circumstances.

3. Try To Prequalify For A Mortgage.

Even before you start your search, go to one or two local banks and see whether you can be prequalified. Although the bank will not give written confirmation that you will get a specific mortgage until all your finances are verified, it will tell you that you are likely to qualify for a mortgage of a certain amount. This knowledge can help you as you begin your house hunt.

4. Decide What You're Looking For In A Home.

It's important to make a list of the features you want in a house and prioritize them. Unless you're purchasing this house alone, your partner or spouse will have to do the same. Together, you can settle on your final priority list. It's easy to be sidetracked by the less important amenities of a house if you haven't put in some fore-thought.

If you are using a broker, make sure he or she knows your priorities and price range and will focus on the right areas when looking through the multiple-listings services or real estate ads. Even though brokers can cut down on your legwork, remember that they are paid a commission from the sale by the seller. This means you should filter all information from the broker with the knowledge that he or she is acting on behalf of the seller.

5. Negotiate The Price.

Finally, you've found your dream house. Now comes the tricky part. How much should you offer? Obviously, you know the asking price. Discuss the following points with the broker:

- **The asking price.** Is it in line with prices in the area for similar homes?

- **The condition of the home.** You should get a professional inspection of the home before you make an offer, particularly with an older house. If it needs significant repairs—new roof, new plumbing, new furnace—you may not want to make an offer. On the other hand, you can try to negotiate a lower price or get the current owner to make the repairs before the sale.

- **Length of time on the market.** If it has been for sale for more than six months, the seller may be eager to accept a lower offer.

- **The neighbors.** They can be a great source of inside information. They know why the seller is selling and whether the seller may be particularly motivated to sell. Check them out.

- **Are there any outstanding offers?** There may be an existing offer to buy the home with the condition that the offerer sell his or her house first. Conditional offers put you in competition with someone else for the same property, so you may have to make a slightly higher offer. However, coming in just under a conditional offer can be attractive to a motivated seller if you can close right away.

After you and the broker have written up your offer, or bid, he or she will deliver it to the seller. It may be accepted, rejected, or countered by the seller asking for a higher price or some other change in terms. This is when the bargaining begins. Negotiating is a skill, but the most useful thing you can do is figure out what is important to the other person. There is no magic formula for positioning yourself in a negotiation. The more information you can find out about the seller, the more able you will be to structure an offer that looks like a good deal. However, it is a two-way street, so be flexible.

Generally, you should make an offer that is 15 percent lower than the asking price. It's always better to make a lower offer, have the seller make a counter offer, then make an offer that the seller immediately snaps up. Remember, don't reveal too much about what you're willing to pay the broker. He or she is obligated to pass on all information to the seller.

Once your offer is accepted, the real work begins. Experienced home buyers often say that the closing process is the most difficult part of the transaction. Just remember that countless home buyers have gone through the same process and survived. And you're not alone—you can talk to your broker, banker, and attorney to help you get through the closing.

After you and the seller have agreed on the purchase price, here's what you have to do:

1. Make a cash down payment. This can be as little as $1,000, but is more often 10 to 20 percent of the purchase price. This money goes into an escrow account until the closing.

2. Arrange for an inspection covering pests, construction, and environmental factors. Specify the dates by which the inspection reports are to be ready. If the inspection uncovers something serious, it could permit you to back out of the deal without losing your deposit.

3. Apply for a mortgage.

6. Obtain A Mortgage.

Once you and the seller have agreed upon a price and have signed the sales agreement, it's time for you to secure a loan. Be prepared to bring the following detailed financial information to the lender:

- Social Security numbers for you and your spouse if both of you are applying for the loan

- copies of your checking and savings account statements for the past six months

- evidence of other assets such as CDs, bonds, stocks, mutual funds
- recent paycheck stubs or statements
- a list of all credit card account numbers and the approximate monthly amount owed on each
- a list of account numbers and balances due on outstanding loans such as car and student loans
- copies of income-tax statements for the past two years
- the name and address of someone who can verify your employment

You should be familiar with some common types of mortgage before you shop for a loan. Each has advantages, and disadvantages, depending on your income level, the length of time you plan to own the home, and other factors. Ask your lender to explain each option before you make a decision.

Fixed-Rate Mortgage

With fixed-rate or conventional mortgages, the interest rate stays the same for the term of the mortgage, generally fifteen or thirty years.

> **Advantage:** Your payment is a stable monthly budget expense.

> **Disadvantage:** Interest rates tend to be higher on fixed-rate loans than they are on other loans—at least initially.

Adjustable-Rate Mortgage (ARM)

With this type of loan, your interest rate and monthly payments usually start out lower than with a fixed-rate mortgage. However, your rate and payment can change either up or down as often as once or twice a year. The adjustment is usually tied to a financial index such as the U.S. Treasury Securities Index. Typically, there is an annual adjustment cap of 2 percent and a lifetime adjustment cap of 6 percent.

> **Advantage:** With an ARM, you may be able to afford a more expensive home because your initial rate and payment will be lower.

> **Disadvantage:** The possibility of upwards adjustments can price the loan payments out of your range.

Government-Insured Mortgages

The federal government backs two types of mortgages: the Federal Housing Authority (FHA) and the Department of Veteran Affairs

(VA). The government insures the lender against loss in case the home buyer defaults on the loan. The FHA program was set up to put homes within the reach of lower-income people. The VA program was set up as a benefit to armed services personnel. With an FHA-insured mortgage, you can purchase your home with as little as 3 percent down. With a VA-insured mortgage, you can purchase your home with nothing down.

Assumable Or Nonassumable

You may find a home with a mortgage loan you can assume (take over) from the previous owner. This means that the bank or other lender is willing to transfer its old loan on the home to you, sometimes at the same interest rate, sometimes at a different interest rate.

> **Advantage**: This can be a wonderful bargain, depending on interest rates. Loan paperwork usually is not complicated, so the closing is often quicker.

> **Disadvantage:** Because the seller is usually liable on the note if you should default, sellers are less willing to negotiate a lower purchase price.

In addition to deciding which mortgage is right for you, you also must decide whether to use a mortgage broker. A mortgage broker represents many different lenders and can get you the lowest available rate in your area. Using a broker can be a convenient way to shop for the best rate. If you have a less-than-stellar credit history, however, you should approach a local bank or credit union. Typically, these institutions are more flexible and may be willing to give you a mortgage because of your previous relationship with the bank.

Here's a worksheet to help you figure out the mortgage amount you can afford:

How Much Of A Mortgage Should You Qualify For?		
	Example	You
Line 1. Monthly payment you can afford (Example: $700 from "How Much Can You Afford" Chart)	$ 700.00	
Line 2. Annual property tax and hazard (Example: $1,900 + $350 = $2,250)	$ 2,250.00	
Line 3. Divide Line 2 by 12 (Example: $2,250 : 12 = $187.50)	$ 187.50	
Line 4. Subtract Line 3 from Line 1 (Example: $700 - $187.50 = $512.50)	$ 512.50	
Line 5. Factor from "Mortgage Factors" Chart (Example: 7% mortgage for 30 years = 150.3)		
Line 6. Multiply Line 4 by Line 5 to determine the approximate mortgage you should qualify for. (Example: $512.50 x 150.3 = $77,028.00).	$77,029.00	

How Much Cash You'll Need To Have

Even though the money you get from the lender will probably cover the majority of the purchase price, you still have to come up with cash for the earnest money, the down payment, and the closing costs, which include a variety of fees.

Earnest Money

When you make an offer on a home, the seller will probably require a deposit as proof that your offer is serious. The seller wants a deposit because the house will be taken off the market once a purchase agreement is signed. This earnest money is held by the seller's broker in an escrow account. If your offer is accepted, your deposit will be put toward part of the down payment or closing costs. If your offer is rejected, the broker will return your deposit.

The Down Payment
The lender will expect you to pay a percentage of the home's price as a down payment. The higher your down payment, the lower the amount of your mortgage loan and corresponding monthly payments or closing costs. If your offer is rejected, the broker will return your deposit.

Closing Costs
These can average 3 to 5 percent of the price of your home. They can include mortgage fees and other expenses.

Application Fee
This charge covers the initial processing costs and the checking of your credit report. It is negotiable. There may be a separate charge of $15 or $20 for the actual credit report.

Title Search And Title Insurance
This charge covers the cost of the title search—examining the public record to confirm ownership of the real estate. It also covers the cost of a title policy, which insures the policyholder for a specific amount against any loss caused by discrepancies in the title to the property. Ask the company carrying the present policy on the house if it can issue your policy at a reissue rate. You could save up to 70 percent of what it would cost for a new policy.

In addition to the title policy, title companies offer a fee policy to cover the differences between the amount of the mortgage and the purchase price of the home.

Most title insurance policies cover liens that exist before you buy (or refinance) your home. Subsequent liens, from either your original purchase mortgage or a home-equity loan, are not covered. When you finish repaying your home loan(s), be sure to obtain— from your county clerk's office or the local agency housing real estate records—a document confirming your lender's removal of its lien against your home.

Attorney's Fees
The lender usually will charge you for fees paid to the lawyer or company that conducts the closing for the lender. Typically, the closing will occur at the office of the lender's attorney. You should have your own attorney to represent you at all stages of the transaction.

Loan-Origination Fees And Points
The origination fee is charged for the lender's work in evaluating and preparing your mortgage loan. Not all lenders charge origination fees. If yours does, this may be a negotiable item. Points are

prepaid finance charges imposed by the lender at closing to increase the lender's yield beyond the stated interest rate on the mortgage note. One point equals 1 percent of the loan amount. For example, one point of a $75,000 loan would be $750. Points and origination fees may be deductible on your income tax return if you itemize deductions. See IRS Publication 936, Home Mortgage Interest Deduction.

Generally, points and origination fees can be deducted in the first year on original mortgages but not on refinancings. For refinancings, the deduction must be spread over the life of the mortgage.

Points and origination fees sometimes can be financed by adding them to the loan amount. But if you refinance again, you can deduct rather than amortize the remainder of the points you paid on the previous refinancing. If you've refinanced twice but didn't deduct the points from the first refinancing, file an amended tax return to capture the deduction.

Appraisal Fee

The lender orders an appraisal to make sure that the fair-market value of the property equals or exceeds the amount of the loan.

Additionally, you may have a fee for a VA or FHA loan, your own attorney's costs, and private mortgage insurance.

The Closing

Even if you've used a broker or attorney to help you with your contract, you still have to pay attention to the details of the process. You should mark a calendar so you don't forget any important dates. Make sure you talk regularly to your attorney, broker, or the seller.

Also, verify that the contract is very specific so that you won't be disappointed or surprised when you do your final walk-through inspection prior to closing. Obviously, the contract will include the price agreed upon, but it should also specify which items the seller has agreed to leave in the house. Any items not listed cannot be presumed to be part of the sale. You'd be amazed at the items that buyers and sellers forget.

The closing can be a nerve-racking experience, especially the first time you go through it. You will feel that you're signing a thousand documents and half your life away. Stay calm. If you've done your homework along the way, the process will go smoothly, and in the end, you will be a home owner. It's by far one of the most satisfying material possessions you can ever hope for!

Used with permission from *Your Financial Guide* by Ray Martin
(Macmillian, 1996)

A mortgage broker helps people find and secure the best mortgage rate the same way a real estate broker finds them the best house. They are similar in that both may have insider information not available to you. In the end, both should save you time and money and serve as negotiators who speed up the process of buying a house.

What Is A Mortgage Broker?

A mortgage broker does what you would do if you had the time, resources, and tolerance for bureaucracy. The best brokers are actually well-trained financial analysts who will listen to your needs, weigh the statistical data, and shop the portfolios of two dozen or so lending institutions to obtain the best mortgage deal for you. What does it cost to use a mortgage broker? Most brokers fees (generally between 1 percent and 3 percent of the cost of the house) are not paid by you, but by the lending institution where the mortgage is issued. The mortgage broker will explain that the bank pays for these services, not you. Although this is true, most banks pass on most or all of this cost to you at closing. If your home costs $50,000, the fee to the mortgage broker can be from $500 to $1,500. Like all services, you need to calculate whether a mortgage broker is worthwhile. Do time and convenience outweigh the cost to you? If the broker can find or negotiate an interest rate that you would not have known about, this service can prove to be an asset. Check with friends and family. If they've purchased a home recently, they may already know where to find the best rate around. The lending institution does have to be located in the same vicinity as your prospective house.

Continuing Your Financial Education

We've come a long way together, haven't we? At this point, our dearest wish is that you feel an inch or two better about how to approach your financial life. You now have the basic tools to master this money thing forever.

This is s a terribly exciting time for the world of finance. As you read this, two far-reaching developments are proceeding. First, the stock market has elected to drop fractions and adapt the decimal system for its stock quotes—a move intended to make investing more user friendly. The second major development is in the area of banking. Legislative blocks initiated in the 1930s to exclude the banking industry from any significant involvement in investing have been cleared. Look for major alliances between the investment, insurance, and banking industries in the coming years. What this potentially means to you is that banks will have the ability to become one-stop financial centers. Imagine the possibility of being able to add a mutual fund and check its progress via on-line banking.

Understand that whether you go on to become the chairman of a multibillion dollar corporation with a seven-figure salary or (an even tougher job) the parent of college-bound children, you probably will have to deal with money on some level almost every day for the rest of your life.

Continue to embrace the Rookie's Five Golden Rules. Again, they are:

1. Get a financial religion.
2. Emotion is the enemy.
3. Your budget will set you free.
4. Keep your eye on the ball.
5. Debt is a cancer.

If you get into trouble, go back and review the steps in the *Manage-to-Grow Money System*. It will help you get back on track. And when dealing with loved ones and money, be gentle. In the end, the former is far more important than the latter.

Also, consider applying the principles of environmental conservation to your financial behavior: *Use only what you must and replace what you can*. Don't stand in front of the sink brushing your teeth with the water running; don't cruise the malls looking for ways to spend money. Your resources, natural or financial, warrant your protection.

Finally, here is the secret no one tells you: Money is fun! Handling money is an intriguing sport that you should never stop following. To help you do that, here is an extremely prejudiced list of the best resources for rookies. These publications, programs, and writers were chosen because they are experts in their field and they make the subject of money fascinating.

Best Financial Newspaper
The Wall Street Journal

Best Financial Magazine
Money Magazine

Best Financial Writers To Look For
Gary Belsky, *Money* Magazine
Cynthia Crossen, *The Wall Street Journal*
Christine Dugas, *USA Today*

Best Columnists To Look For
Jane Bryant Quinn
Barbara Geddes Quint

Best Financial Television Show (Cable)
CNBC's "Moneytalk"

Best Financial Television Segment (Network)
NBC's "Today" (Money segment with Ray Martin)

Best Financial Television Segment (Cable)
CNN's "Dollars & Sense"

Best Financial Television Show That's An Acquired Taste
"The Wall Street Week"

Best Financial Radio Network
Bloomberg Information Radio

Best Financial Software
Intuit's Quicken (any version)
Ernst & Young's Prosper (for investing)

Best Financial Books
Anything published by The Wall Street Journal
Anything published by Ernst & Young
One Up On Wall Street by Peter Lynch
The Beardstown Ladies' Common-Sense Investment Guide by The Beardstown Ladies

Best Financial Reference Book
Barron's Finance & Investment Handbook

Notes:

Notes:

Notes:

Notes:

Notes:

Notes: